John Abbott

After a varied career as an actor in theatre, film and television, John Abbott became a teacher of acting. He was Head of Acting at the ArtsEd School of Acting in London, where he taught Shakespeare, Stand Up and Improvisation, and directed many projects and productions. His previous books are *The Improvisation Book* and *Improvisation in Rehearsal*, both published by Nick Hern Books.

Other Titles in this Series

ACTING AND REACTING *Tools for the Modern Actor*
Nick Moseley

ACTIONS: THE ACTORS' THESAURUS
Marina Caldarone and Maggie Lloyd-Williams

THE ACTOR AND THE TARGET
Declan Donnellan

BEYOND STANISLAVSKY
The Psycho-Physical Approach to Actor Training
Bella Merlin

THE COMPLETE STANISLAVSKY TOOLKIT
Bella Merlin

DIFFERENT EVERY NIGHT *Freeing the Actor*
Mike Alfreds

DRAMA GAMES FOR CLASSROOMS AND WORKSHOPS
Jessica Swale

DRAMA GAMES FOR DEVISING
Jessica Swale

DRAMA GAMES FOR THOSE WHO LIKE TO SAY NO
Chris Johnston

FINDING YOUR VOICE *A Step-by-Step Guide for Actors*
Barbara Houseman

HOUSE OF GAMES *Making Theatre from Everyday Life*
Chris Johnston

THE IMPROVISATION BOOK
How to Conduct Successful Improvisation Sessions
John Abbott

THE IMPROVISATION GAME
Discovering the Secrets of Spontaneous Performance
Chris Johnston

IMPROVISATION IN REHEARSAL
John Abbott

SO YOU WANT TO BE AN ACTOR?
Prunella Scales and Timothy West

TACKLING TEXT [AND SUBTEXT] *A Step-by-Step Guide for Actors*
Barbara Houseman

THROUGH THE BODY *A Practical Guide to Physical Theatre*
Dymphna Callery

WHY IS THAT SO FUNNY? *A Practical Exploration of Physical Comedy*
John Wright

John Abbott

THE ACTING BOOK

NICK HERN BOOKS
London
www.nickhernbooks.co.uk

A NICK HERN BOOK

The Acting Book
first published in Great Britain in 2012
by Nick Hern Books Limited
14 Larden Road, London W3 7ST

Cover designed by Peter Bennett

Typeset by Nick Hern Books
Printed and bound in Great Britain
by T.J. International, Padstow, Cornwall

A CIP catalogue record for this book is available
from the British Library

ISBN 978 1 84842 144 8

MIX
Paper from
responsible sources
FSC® C013056
FSC
www.fsc.org

Contents

For David
and Susan
Gardner

Author's Note

I MUST HAVE WORKED WITH THOUSANDS OF ACTORS OVER the years and they are an amazing bunch of people. I would like to mention them all by name, but that's impossible, of course. So here are a few of the actors who have made me sit up, listen and want to be like them:

Philip Voss, who made me understand the difference between amateur and professional acting when he shouted 'Zounds' as the dying Mercutio (Ipswich Arts Theatre, 1963).

Chris Crooks, my drama school (and life-long) buddy whose camel was legendary. As was his Hamlet (Central School of Speech and Drama, 1967–69, and The Century Theatre, 1971).

Ian Richardson, whose passion, voice and commitment to performing enthralled me and audiences alike (Royal Shakespeare Company, 1972).

Lawrence Werber, strong, steadfast and honorable both as a friend and as an actor (Phoebus Cart, 1991).

And Mark Rylance, who has stunned a whole generation of actors and theatregoers (Phoebus Cart and Sonnet Walks, 1990s).

Also, I've got to mention my kids, Nick and Katie, who had to grow up with an actor dad. 'What does your father do for a living?' asked a teacher. 'He goes for interviews,' said Katie. Neither Nick nor Katie ever wanted to go on the stage or anywhere near it! (Although Nick likes to build film sets.)

Finally, never-ending thanks to Nick Hern for his rigorous (but always apposite) editorial comments; Matt Applewhite for conversations and advice, and without whom this book wouldn't exist; Jodi Gray for making the pages look great; and to all the rest of the people at Nick Hern Books for their various book-publishing talents and friendly faces.

John Abbott

Foreword

THIS BOOK IS FOR PEOPLE WHO ARE INTERESTED IN HOW actors prepare for performances.

For teachers it is a recipe book of techniques and processes.

For directors it could also be an insight into the way that actors think.

And for actors it is an introduction to some new techniques and a reminder of techniques they may once have learned but have long since forgotten.

~

This book is about the way we teach acting at ArtsEd, the drama school where I've worked for the past twelve years. It started life as a handbook for our students. A checklist of taught techniques. But people outside the school discovered it, found it useful and asked if they could have a copy. At that point it was simply a summary of the training, because the exercises were not described in detail. There was no need to do so because the students had been taught them in class. Then my publisher, Nick Hern, who described the handbook as 'a fast-forward acting course', asked me to retain the outline structure but fill in the detail. The result is this book.

Its main purpose is to describe how to support and strengthen an actor's artistic intentions and build their confidence. It describes various ways to analyse a text, create a character and develop character relationships. It includes a range of rehearsal techniques and improvisations, and it introduces an assortment of exercises to stimulate the actor's imagination.

But basically it is an outline of some of the things that actors can do to create memorable performances that will captivate their audiences.

Introduction

'All Art is Useless'

GOOD OLD OSCAR WILDE. YOU'VE GOT TO LOVE HIM. SOME of the things he said just hang there in your mind and make you wish you'd said them yourself.

He's undeniably right, of course: Art is useless because it doesn't 'do' anything. But after smiling at his cheek and admiring his wit, you realise that he's making a positive statement about Art. He actually loves the uselessness of it. It doesn't help you gather food. It doesn't keep you warm and dry. It doesn't make you healthy and strong. It doesn't keep body and soul together.

Or does it?

Possibly the earliest form of Art was storytelling. Who knows? It could arguably have been cave painting, but for that you need to have invented some sort of paint and devised a way of applying it to the walls of the cave. For storytelling you don't need to have invented anything at all. Except language. And perhaps a story. I can imagine these cavemen sitting around the fire after a hunting trip and telling everyone what happened during the hunt. They probably embellished the details and exaggerated the characters just like we do today: 'So-and-so was really brave. He grabbed the mammoth by his tail and wouldn't let go'… 'And then What's-his-name fell over a tree trunk as usual and we all laughed'… 'Yes, but Who's-it was absolutely useless. He's been in a dreamworld ever since he fell in love with Her-over-there.'

And you know how it is when you tell a good story: you want to show people what happened, so you get up and start acting out various incidents. In all probability the people in the hunt got up and started acting out whole scenes together. And, of course, a really good story could be told again and again, and each time they told it they would have got better and better at acting out the good bits. Then some people listening to the story may have wanted to tell it to a completely different group of people, so they had to tell it in the third person. And as they acted it out maybe they pretended to be the people who were originally in the hunt. Some of those old cave-dwellers may have become really good storytellers. And some others probably become expert actors as they acted out the incidents for their cave-dwelling audiences.

You see what I'm getting at, don't you?

Drama. Theatre. Acting.

And what makes a good storyteller? Well, for a start, it's someone who can make the characters in the story clear, unique and detailed, because everyone is different, and human beings have always been interested in the way that other human beings behave. But a good storyteller is also someone who makes the story come alive for the listeners so their imaginations can become fully engaged. Maybe the best storyteller is someone who performs the acted-out bits as realistically as possible, and who brings truth to the emotional experience of the characters, because that makes the listeners think deeply about what it is to be human. They may even ponder philosophical questions like 'Who are we?' and 'What is the meaning of life?'

As far as I can tell, people who are good at acting things out have always tried to make their acting seem real. Even good joke-tellers in the pub will often start off by making you think they are telling a true story about themselves or about a friend of theirs. A clown spraying fake tears over the first few rows of the audience will get more laughs if he has an inner truth of sadness as he does it. If you look at photographs of Henry

Irving, the first actor to be knighted, he used extreme physical gestures when he performed: his hands are stretched sideways, his fingers splayed and his eyes are wild with emotion. But strangely enough, all the reviewers at the time commended him on his naturalism. So what was going on? Well, I think Henry Irving must have had that 'inner truth' as he acted. Don't forget that theatres were lit by gaslight in those days, and it must have been pretty hard for the people in the upper gallery to see the actors' faces. Perhaps Irving used exaggerated gestures in order to project his character's inner life to the people in the gods. And look at Shakespeare, who was making theatre four hundred years ago. In Hamlet's speech to the troupe of players visiting Elsinore, he asks them to hold 'the mirror up to nature' when they act. In other words, to be natural. I suspect that naturalism has always been at the core of great acting. It's instinctive to act with truth because stories always work better that way.

A hundred years ago along came Konstantin Stanislavsky, the godfather of drama training, who spent his life analysing and quantifying the artistic instincts of the best actors, so that all the other actors could do what they do. Since then there have been loads of different 'methods', 'techniques' and 'cults' about actor training, but they all go back to Stanislavsky in the end. And the whole thing is quite simple.

- Analyse the text and examine the details so you know what the writer had in mind.
- Create a character that both the actor and the audience can believe in.
- Then perform the play as truthfully as possible, with all the actors listening and responding to each other.

That's all there is to it. Thanks, Konstantin.

But, of course, that's like saying that all Michelangelo had to do was find a nice piece of marble, chip out the shape he wanted and smooth off the surface!

When I started to teach acting, I read loads of books, from Stanislavsky to Michael Chekhov, through Grotowski, Augusto Boal, Keith Johnstone and others. I even read David Mamet, who thinks that actor training is rubbish and all you have to do is to stand still and say the lines as written. ('Know your lines and don't bump into the furniture,' said Noël Coward. But he was joking!)

In order to create my first classes, I used bits and pieces from all the books I'd read, but as the years passed I began to adapt other people's exercises and invent techniques of my own. Without noticing it I had developed my own style of teaching. It was the same with directing. To start with I used all sorts of tried-and-tested rehearsal techniques, anything that might solve a problem. Stanislavsky. Michael Chekhov. Mike Alfreds. It took me ages to get my head around 'units and objectives'. Everyone I met seemed to have a different theory about what they were, so I finally came up with a version that seemed to work for me and I started teaching that. Some people got it and some didn't. And it was especially hard for people who had been taught a different version by previous drama teachers.

Then I started using improvisation in rehearsals to create characters and relationships. Most people loved it, but others just wanted to be told their 'moves' so they could decide how they were going to say their lines.

Also, I discovered that some people loved to research and find out as much as they could about the background of the play and the characters, while others hardly bothered at all. They just used their 'feelings' about these things. Their instincts.

Some people liked to 'action' the text, while others loved the Meisner technique. Some people used the study of animals to create their characters, while others put on their costumes to see how particular clothing affected their character's physicality.

I realised that some things work for some people and other things work for others. And I realised that some things work on some plays and other things work on other plays. Or that some things work with a certain bunch of actors and other things with other bunches. There is no method for acting that is universal and foolproof, despite what some gurus may postulate, because all plays are different. All characters are different. And all actors are different. They are creative artists, so what can you expect? Imagine if everyone painted like Hockney, how boring the art world would be. I mean, I love David Hockney, but imagine how it would be if all artists made pictures like him. No Tracey Emin. No Banksy. No Lucian Freud or Lowry or Francis Bacon…

Most of these people, including David Hockney, went to art school where they learned how to reflect on their artistic vision as well as how to manipulate the tools of their trade. With the proper training in artistic possibilities combined with an understanding of practical techniques, they were able to give life to their unique vision.

For me, that's what drama training is all about for actors. As I've just tried to show, acting is pretty straightforward in outline, but in detail it's as complicated and varied as the personalities of all the people who act.

Techniques

In this book I will be talking about both analytical and artistic techniques, and explaining how they are mutually beneficial. Actors are artists, and like all artists they have to combine a technical understanding of their craft with an unbridled, free-flowing, creative instinct.

Where I teach we have struggled to come to terms with how to combine our training in the intellectual analysis of a text with the free-flowing responsive methods of the Meisner technique. And at first glance they seem to be at odds. But if you look at the diagrammatic representation of the yin and the yang you will find that it is made of two shapes: one is jet black with a white dot in the middle and the other is pure white with a black dot in the middle. They are total opposites.

But each shape, unsatisfactory as it is in isolation, fits snugly against the other to create a perfect circle. And the circle has traditionally been used as the diagrammatic representation of harmony and completeness.

So while we try to understand and develop the artistic intentions of our student actors, we also introduce them to a whole suite of productive methods to help them realise their inner creative vision. Some of the methods we use are tried and tested and will be familiar; a few of them are invented; and others are still in the experimental stage. But all these methods can sometimes be useful, although not for everyone all the time. The best advice I can give to anyone using this book is to try things out and see what happens. I once suggested to a very experienced actor that we 'hot-seated' his character, which means the actor has to answer random questions in character, without preparation. 'Oh, John, I don't need to do that! That's drama-school stuff,' he said. 'Try it,' I said. 'Okaaay,' he answered with a resigned sigh.

He began answering my questions with a certain reluctance, but after a while he became more animated, and I could see his character start to come to life. When we finished he was bubbling over with enthusiasm. 'That was great,' he said. 'I really enjoyed it. I never realised that my character…', etc., etc., and I couldn't stop him talking for ages.

So my advice is:

Use the exercises with enthusiasm and you might be surprised by the results.

Subtext

The subtext is basically the desires, thoughts and emotions that a character might feel, even when they are having an apparently innocuous conversation. Sometimes in real life people find it hard to express what they really feel, either because it would be socially unacceptable for them to do so or because they don't want anyone else to know too much about them. So they use half-truths and evasions, or talk about other things to disguise their inner feelings. And these inner feelings are the subtext. Writers like Chekhov and Harold Pinter have consciously used subtext when writing dialogue, and the word 'subtext' is often used to refer literally to the hidden thoughts behind the text of a play. But I will be using the term in a broader context, meaning the unspoken thoughts behind any spoken words, be they in a play, a film, or in real life.

Of course, an actor has to have a good understanding of their character's subtext, but the biggest danger is to try to 'act out' the subtext so it is clear to the audience. In real life, people usually try to keep their subtext hidden. It's there but you can't perceive it. In fact, people are often desperately trying to conceal their thoughts and emotions. And that is how actors should use subtext. They should understand it, know it, feel it, and then suppress it. You could say, 'Why bother with it in the first place if you are going to keep it hidden?', but that would be underestimating the audience's perceptive skills. If an actor feels an emotion, the audience will pick up on it, however deeply the emotion is hidden, and that will make them feel involved. But if you bring the subtext to the surface and spoon-feed it to the audience then you are not allowing them to participate and they will soon lose interest.

The bottom line is:

Keep the subtext 'sub'.
Don't act it, or it will just become a new 'text'.

Lonelyhearts

One of the first things our students at ArtsEd do is to create characters from scratch. They start with very little information and then, through a process of observation and improvisation, they each develop a fully rounded, truthful character. These lonelyhearts sessions were originally devised by Jane Harrison, who based some of the creative process on the techniques of Mike Leigh, but over the years these sessions have developed into the series of exercises described in Chapter 2. Thanks to Jane Harrison for describing this to me, but also, many thanks to Charlie Barker, who is the Head of Acting for the ArtEd BA in Musical Theatre, because she added her own particular flavour to this process and has allowed me to include some additional material which is all her own.

Improvisation

There are many forms of improvisation, from cooking to playing jazz to performing in front of an audience. Improvisation just means that people are making things up on the spot without any preparation or preconception.

The improvisations that I talk about in this book are improvisations to help actors explore various aspects of a script, and as such they should always be played truthfully. They are not about entertaining the other actors, impressing the director or being funny. They are a means of exploiting the actors' ability to 'pretend' in order to help them develop their characters, explore relationships within the script and ultimately present a multilayered version of life in their performances.

At ArtsEd we teach the students how to improvise dialogue both truthfully and creatively. It's not as simple as it seems, because actors can often produce very bland conversations when you take away their instinct to entertain. Their improvisations may be very realistic but they are not learning anything new. So we teach them how to replace that instinct to entertain with something more creative. They learn how to make up stories about their characters and build complex relationships by making on-the-spot decisions without any fear. There is a brief outline of this in Chapter 10, but you will find an in-depth description of our improvisation training in *The Improvisation Book*.

In short, it is important to remember:

Keep the improvisations real. They are to help the actors, not to entertain the audience.

Meisner

Sanford Meisner developed a technique to help actors connect with each other and respond 'in the moment'. This is the basis of good acting because it tells the story with truth and dynamism, and because the performances are being created as the audience watches.

The Meisner technique as outlined in Chapters 11 and 12 would not be considered to be pure Meisner by some practitioners. Our second-year acting tutor, Aileen Gonsalves, has developed and refined the technique in order to make her own explorations and to solve her own rehearsal challenges. So, although her process is based on Meisner, it is, in fact, her own interpretation of the technique. I would like to thank her for the time she spent giving me a detailed description of her work, and to point out that Chapters 11 and 12 were devised and written by both of us.

Film and Television

At ArtsEd we give the students a very thorough training in acting for film and television because we realise the abundance of professional opportunities in this area. More and more British actors are getting work in American films and television series;

there are a growing number of low-budget films being made by young directors; and the internet is an open house for new creative ideas for both drama and comedy. Of course, acting is acting, and a lot of the basic training we give applies to both stage and screen, so I have tried to describe the techniques and exercises in this book in a way that is not specific to either theatre or film. Sometimes this may sound a bit heavy-handed and awkward. For instance, rather than talking about 'plays' or 'film scripts', I use 'scripts' or 'texts' as cover-all words. On a few occasions the techniques are specific to theatre, particularly since film and television work can often have a rather skimpy rehearsal schedule. But none of the exercises are specific to acting for the camera. That is another book.

Shakespeare

I have included some quotations from Shakespeare as a fun way of introducing each chapter of this book. It's amazing how he has something to say about almost any subject you can imagine! But I have also used references to popular Shakespeare plays and characters when I need to illustrate particular points. I've done this because, of all the playwrights that I could have chosen, Shakespeare is the one that most people will be familiar with.

I have also used Chekhov's plays to illustrate points, as well as American plays and films from the 1950s, because the writers and actors in both those eras were experimenting with naturalism. This makes them ideal vehicles for exercises in exploration and discovery.

The Confidence Trick

I suppose the most important aspect of our training at ArtsEd is positivity. It's a belief that the students we teach already have the right instincts and talent for acting, so all we have to do is to help them believe in themselves and introduce them to various techniques to realise their artistic vision. They know how they want to act: they sometimes just don't know how to go about it.

The trouble with acting is that the actor can't see the results of his or her work unless they are making a film, and even then their judgement is clouded because they usually just focus on their own performance. As an actor they are part of a creative team, but it is very difficult for them to have an objective view of their contribution to the play or the film. They are each cogs in the creative wheel and all they can do is to 'feel' how their performance has gone. Perhaps they can judge from the audience reaction, but even that is subjective. Laughter from the audience may convey a certain amount of enjoyment, but what happens when an actor is playing in a tragedy? Best to hope there will be no laughter. No, apart from relying on their own instincts and feelings, actors have to depend on the feedback of trusted professionals. Directors. Teachers. Voice coaches. People with an objective view who can help actors visualise their performances and understand the effect they have on an audience. I don't mean, though, that a director or a teacher should beat an actor into submission by relentlessly criticising their work and overpowering them with their own methodology. On the contrary, at ArtsEd we believe that an actor needs to understand what is *right* about their work, and if they understand that, then the *wrong* will just disappear.

I first met Jane Harrison when she was teaching on a foundation course in acting at the City and Islington College, and I was amazed when she kept telling her students that they were brilliant. I'd never come across such positivity in my life. But the funny thing was, her students just got better and better. Her positivity worked. At first I thought it was a trick and that she didn't really mean it. But she did. She genuinely believed her students were brilliant.

And of course it was true. They were. People are brilliant if they are allowed to be. Unfortunately they lose their sparkle if they are constantly being degraded and abused. Kick a rough diamond around and it stays rough, but if you examine its structure, carefully release its potential, and polish its unique facets, it shines and glitters with a thousand colours.

Of course, there is no point in lying. If an actor is mumbling their lines incoherently, it would be stupid to say, 'That was brilliant, I heard every word.' What good would that do? But if you praise the actor for the insightful depth of character creation (if it's true), and then point out that it works best when the audience can understand the subtleties of dialogue as well as they can understand the subtleties of character, then the actor will automatically want to convey the meaning of every single word. Both Marlon Brando and James Dean were criticised for a certain amount of vocal incoherence in their early work, but if you listen to them from the perspective of the twenty-first century, you realise that, while they were at odds with what was then the accepted method of speaking dialogue, they made sure that the audience understood everything they *wanted* the audience to understand. People accused Marlon Brando of mumbling, but listen again to him in his early films. That's not a mumble: it's his way of investing the written dialogue with the natural rhythms of human speech. If the director Elia Kazan had said to him: 'Marlon, I didn't hear all the words. You're a useless actor. You've got to speak more clearly,' then *On the Waterfront* would have been forgotten long ago.

But he didn't. Kazan gave Brando confidence to explore a new depth of acting while making sure that he was still telling the story with emotional clarity and truth. Kazan focused on the positives. And that's what we do at ArtsEd. That's our technique. It helps the students to believe in themselves. Call it a trick if you like, but it works. It gives them confidence.

It's a confidence trick.

1
Storytelling

HAMLET. ... My lord, you play'd once i' th' university, you say?

POLONIUS. That I did, my lord, and was accounted a good actor.

Hamlet (3.2)

A FEW YEARS AGO I GOT A JOB DIRECTING SECOND-YEAR acting students at the Mountview Academy of Theatre Arts. I had to direct a play and teach the students how to be actors at the same time. The play I chose was *The Vortex* by Noël Coward. It was written in 1924 when Coward was a young man, and it concerns the problems of taking drugs and how your relationship with your parents changes when you leave home. All in all I thought it was a subject that acting students could easily relate to.

At the time I was living in Chiswick, which is in West London. Mountview is in North London, so each day I drove round the North Circular Road on my motorbike to get to work. In his book *Zen and the Art of Motorcycle Maintenance*, Robert Pirsig describes a journey he made both physically, on his motorbike, and philosophically – into his consciousness. He uses a Native American word to describe this journey. He calls it a *Chautauqua*. There appear to be many definitions of the word 'Chautauqua' but I've taken it to mean: 'Philosophical thoughts you have while travelling'. It's a great word.

So anyway, as I was travelling round the North Circular Road I was puzzling over how I could teach these Mountview students to become actors, and I came up with these two thoughts:

> 'Work like a Trojan.
> Play like a child.'

The words kept ringing in my ears.

And as I travelled on between the lanes of crawling cars, other ideas came into my head, so when I got to Mountview I quickly wrote everything down. Later I refined it and reworked it, but essentially the thoughts I had on that journey – my Chautauqua – eventually became what I now call 'The Ego Paradox'. It looks like a poem, but it's not. It's just a set of instructions on how to be an actor.

The Ego Paradox

Work like a ***Trojan***
Play like a ***child***

Have the imagination of a ***poet***
The gusto of an ***abstract expressionist***
And the courage of a ***gambler***

Research like a ***detective***
Experiment like a ***mad scientist***
Think like a ***philosopher***
And practise like a ***magician***

Focus your concentration like an
athlete in the Olympic Games

Believe in yourself as completely as
the President of the United States

And always perform with the
passionate commitment of a
sanctified mystic.

Let me explain.

First of all the title. 'The Ego Paradox'. What's that all about?

It describes the paradox that an actor faces. In order to be able to stand up in front of hundreds of people and have them watch you pretend to be someone else, you have to have a pretty strong sense of who you are. You have to have a strong ego. But on the other hand, when you are playing a role, you have to suppress your own ego and take on the ego of the character you are playing. Therein lies the paradox.

Work like a Trojan
Play like a child

Being an actor is hard work, both physically and mentally, but actors should never lose sight of how childish it is and how much fun it can be. Children take their play very seriously, and so should actors. Work like Trojans? Well, I'd heard the expression before and assumed it meant to work very hard indeed. Anyway, that's what I meant it to mean.

Have the imagination of a poet

Poets let their imaginations float above the common toil of everyday life. Nothing is barred. They keep their minds open so that all sorts of ideas and thoughts can drift in and be enjoyed. They are not afraid to examine their imaginative fantasies and write them down. They daydream creatively and that's something that actors should do. Actors should open their imaginations just like poets.

The gusto of an abstract expressionist

One of the most famous abstract expressionists was the American painter Jackson Pollock. Sometimes they called his pictures 'action paintings', and I'm not surprised. I once saw a film of him working, using all these big tins of liquid paint, which looked like brightly coloured house paint. He laid his canvas flat on the floor and ran around splashing different colours on the canvas straight from the tin. It was like a sort of ballet. His physical movements were part of the action. He dipped and dribbled and swooped and spun with tremendous gusto. The picture sprang into life. Actors should splash their ideas around just like Jackson Pollock splashed his paint around. A bit of red here! Splash! Spin! How about some yellow? Splatter! Swirl! Take big chances. Try out ideas and see what happens. Create with gusto.

The courage of a gambler

Courage comes in many guises. We think of courage being needed in life-or-death situations. Going into battle. Sky-diving off a mountain. Confronting an armed criminal. That sort of thing. But although acting is important, I don't think anyone should risk their lives for it. But money? That's different. I read this story in the papers about a man who sold everything he owned – his house, his car, his furniture, his clothes probably – gathered up all his money and took it to Las Vegas. One evening he went down to the roulette table and put all his cash on the black. This would mean he would either lose everything or he would double it. Whatever happened, it would change his life. As I read about this guy I thought about the moment he put his money down. What courage he must have had. He didn't have to do it. The money was his. He could take it back to England and buy another house. But no! Here goes nothing. Put the money on the black and sweat. Watch the ball whizz around the edge of the roulette wheel. Spin. Whizz. Bounce. Circle. Bounce and bounce. And... Time must have stood still... Where will it rest...? Plop! What a great story, but what *courage*. To risk everything. That is the sort of courage that an actor needs in rehearsal. The courage to lose everything. The courage to fail. (I know you want to know what happened at that roulette wheel. Well... he won!)

Research like a detective

Look for clues. In the script, on the internet, in conversations with other people; they can be anywhere and everywhere. Detectives love to collect clues. They know that the tiniest thing could be important. A strand of hair. A bus ticket to Ruislip. Anything and everything is worth considering. Actors should collect together all the clues they can find, just like a detective. Examine them. Evaluate them. And draw conclusions. Every detail is another part of the jigsaw. The script is full of clues. Look carefully. Some are easy to miss.

Experiment like a mad scientist

'A little of zis blue liquid mixed over a flame viz some phosphorus and a dash of charcoal.' Pop and fizz. It starts to bubble. 'I'll add zis mysterious concoction I made yesterday.' Bubble, bubble, bubble. 'How about putting in some more...?' BANG!!!***!!! Explosion. Hair on end. Blackened face. Insane laughter. 'Ha! Ha! Ha! Zat vas interestink!' The mad scientist creates the elixir of life and drinks it, even though it might turn him into a monster. But at least he tried to make something happen. And his next concoction could make him live for ever, with X-ray eyes and superhuman strength. The mad scientist takes a chance, tries something new and comes up with unexpected results. That's what actors need to do. Experiment.

Think like a philosopher

Philosophers calmly weigh all the facts and theories. They look for connections. They balance one idea against another and come up with innovative conclusions. They attempt to answer impossible questions about existence, truth and art. In their search to bring the bigger picture into focus they ponder every detail. Philosophy is a love of knowledge. A love of wisdom. Philosophers use their intellect in a systematic and reasoned manner, collating and comparing the wisdom of others. That's what actors should do.

Practise like a magician

Magicians will practise a trick over and over again so the audience won't see how it's done. They put a lot of effort into making things look effortless. Like ballet dancers or jugglers, they spend hours and hours in preparation in order to perfect their art and create a few minutes of unforced, confident entertainment. And, let's face it, actors themselves are magicians. They play tricks with the audience's imagination. They make fictitious characters come to life. They conjure up other eras. Other worlds. The audience sits comfortably in a darkened room while the actors take them on exciting journeys. But in order to do all this successfully, actors have to rehearse. They have to practise so the audience doesn't see the mechanics of their conjuring tricks.

Focus your concentration like an athlete in the Olympic Games

Wholehearted concentration produces better results. Athletes focus on the job in hand. They stand at the start of the hundred-metre dash with every ounce of their concentration focused on the finishing line. In their mind's eye they have already won the race. All the surrounding distractions are eliminated in their desire to be at their best for approximately ten seconds. In some events, like the high jump, when every muscle must work perfectly the minute they leave the ground, you often see the athlete physically acting through their movements before they make an attempt. They are imagining success. They are focused. They are concentrating. That's the sort of concentration that actors need when they are rehearsing or performing a scene. It can't be half-hearted. It has to be total. And they need to get into that zone before they start to work.

Believe in yourself as completely as the President of the United States

It doesn't matter who the President is, or in what decade, every single President during my lifetime has had a massively positive sense of self-belief. I suppose they have to or they would never get any votes. The funny thing is, self-belief works. 'To thine own self be true,' says Polonius in Shakespeare's *Hamlet.* And he wasn't wrong. If you believe in yourself and your way of doing things, then other people will often believe in you and admire what you do. We know about creative artists who defied the existing rules and broke new ground with their art. They are the ones who resolutely swam against the tide with a total belief in themselves. And they are the people we remember today. Van Gogh. Bob Dylan. Stravinsky. Ernest Hemingway. Marlon Brando. Innovators all. The people that changed things. Created a new version of their art. If actors can learn to believe in themselves and what they are doing, then everyone else will believe in them too.

Always perform with the passionate commitment of a sanctified mystic

Hah! What does that mean? What's a sanctified mystic when it's at home? Well, I don't know – I made it up. A friend of mine once described himself as an 'astral dervish' and I loved that. Someone whirling through the cosmos, happy and out of control. So during my Chautauqua I was searching for a phrase that was something like an 'astral dervish' and I came up with a 'sanctified mystic'. Sanctified means to make holy, and a mystic is a person who seeks the truth of life. All I know is that people who are involved in these things always speak with a passionate gleam in their eyes. They love their own version of the truth and want to share it with the rest of us. They are committed to their beliefs in such a way that they seem to have a steel-blue electric aura. That's the sort of commitment an actor needs. The passionate commitment of a sanctified mystic! What can I say? Go for it!

Trust

A bunch of actors get together to rehearse a play. Several weeks later the fruits of their collaboration are presented to an audience without a safety net. That's scary.

Often the actors don't know each other before they start rehearsals, and yet they have to explore their own emotional life as part of the creative process. Sometimes during rehearsals an actor will need to be emotionally naked in front of the rest of the cast. Nothing hidden. No privacy. Most people would be unable to do that, but actors do it because they have learned to trust each other.

The way most people learn to trust others is by talking about themselves, listening to each other and trying to find some common ground. As someone begins to reveal details about their life to another person, then the other person feels confident to disclose details of their own life. It becomes a game of mutual acceptance. If you know that your companion cries at emotional stories, then you don't feel embarrassed when your own tears start to flow. Sharing personal experiences leads to a deeper mutual understanding, and that eventually develops into a reciprocal trust. We've all done it. We all want it. But for actors, trust is an essential commodity. It's part of their job.

Right at the start of our training at ArtsEd we embark on a storytelling project. This culminates in a devised performance piece created from stories that the actors have told each other about their own lives. Each actor has the opportunity to tell one or more stories. When several actors have had similar experiences they work together on a collaborative section within the presentation. Stories that have a more sensitive or emotional content are sometimes presented in a more abstract manner through movement, sound or poetry. The results are always fascinating. Often artistic. Sometimes incomprehensible. And, for the actors involved, deeply moving.

But the purpose is not to put on a show. The true purpose lies in what's revealed during the process. The exploration of emotions and the 'self' is a vital part of an actor's resources. As each student tells the others about incidents in their lives, the group begins to understand the variety of human experience. They all have a common ambition. They want to be actors. But that doesn't mean they are all the same by any means. They come from vastly different backgrounds, and their life experiences are varied and diverse. Some of the stories are really unexpected, leaving the other students gobsmacked. At first there is a reluctance to share the personal details of their lives, but once the floodgates start to open, the stories pour out and the group trust begins to build.

But, of course, you can't just ask people to talk about themselves without giving them the right sort of supportive environment; otherwise many of them will just clam up.

Storytelling

There are several storytelling games that can ease the actors into this process, and help them to start talking and recognising shared experiences. The first is an adaptation of an Augusto Boal game.

Conform or Die

Several actors walk around the room together, and as they walk they march in step. Military fashion. At the same time, another actor dances around the room, expressing happiness and freedom. As the exercise progresses the marchers become more aggressive in the way they move, even to the extent of making it hard for the dancer to move freely. They can corner the dancer, push her aside or even surround her in a hostile, antagonistic manner. They can then force her to the ground with apparent aggression (no one must get hurt). The dancer can try to get up and dance again, and the same thing happens. Her freedom is restricted. Again she is forced to the ground. And again. Until the

dancer stops trying to dance and has no option but to join in with the marchers. At this point another actor gets up and starts to dance, and the whole exercise is repeated.

When this exercise has finished, the actors discuss what has happened. What did they think it meant? What would they do if it happened to them? Does gender make any difference? What did the participants feel like?

This discussion is wide-ranging, and as it progresses the actors are encouraged to talk about their own personal experiences of individualism, oppression and isolation.

The Drama Triangle – *Part One*

The actors get into groups of three and cast themselves as members of a family. This can be any combination they like. Father, mother and teenager. Teenage boy, teenage girl and grandparent. Husband, wife and brother-in-law. The permutations are endless but there must be family connections within each group, and each person must have a specific position in the family. Having cast themselves in these roles, each actor has to decide on a particular mode of behaviour. One has to be a persecutor, another the victim and the third a rescuer. When they have done this, they improvise a family scene.

In many family situations there is a triangular relationship, where one person persecutes another and a third tries to come to the rescue. For instance, an older brother could persecute a younger brother, and their mother could try to come to the rescue. Or in another situation, the father could be persecuting the mother and it's the child who could try to intervene. There are many variations. Some of which will already be familiar to the actors.

When they do the improvisation it is important that the actors stay true to their designated mode of behaviour. The victim should never try to retaliate, however much they may feel inclined. The victim should remain a victim. The rescuer must try to rescue the situation and not start to persecute the persecutor. And, of course, the persecutor should persecute at all times.

This exercise feels amazingly true to life, and it helps the actors understand that this drama triangle is at the heart of many family situations.

Part Two

After they have done the first improvisation, the actors stay as the same family member, but swap around their modes of behaviour. For instance, it could have been that an older brother was the persecutor, but he now becomes the victim. The mother was the rescuer, but she is now the persecutor, and the younger brother who was the victim the first time round now becomes the rescuer. They then improvise another version of the scene.

When they do this they find that this second improvisation also rings true. The modes of behaviour in a family group are not determined by the specific relationships in the family.

Part Three

The actors still stay as the same family member but they take on the mode of behaviour that they haven't yet tried. This would mean that the mother now becomes the victim, the older brother is the rescuer, and the younger brother has to persecute his mother. Then they improvise another version of the scene.

This third improvisation will demonstrate that this drama triangle is a recognisable scenario whatever the permutation of modes of behaviour.

Discussion

The actors discuss family relationships and the things that were revealed during the improvisations.

The discussion is often quite lively, as the actors recognise aspects of their own lives. This exercise is invaluable in helping the actors start to share their personal experiences of family life with each other. Gradually the walls of inhibition start to crumble.

Stories

Working as a whole group, the actors tell each other stories about their own life experiences.

This can take five or six sessions, depending on the size of the group, and it's important that everybody tells a story. Some of the stories will resonate with other members of the group who have shared similar experiences, while other stories will reveal the unique and varied journeys that each person has made through life up until this point. Of course, it's not easy to open up to relative strangers, but there are a number of support mechanisms to help the actors talk about themselves. Here are some suggestions:

Music

The actors play a piece of music that has a particular significance in their lives. As it plays in the background, they tell the rest of the group why it is important to them.

Music will often stimulate an emotional response and bring half-forgotten memories to the surface. But not only that, music is a great way to bring a group together and create a specific mood.

As you can imagine, this music often becomes part of the final devised piece.

Crossroads

The actors talk about a time when they were at a crossroads in their lives.

This is a time of change. A time when they had to make a decision or a time when a decision was made for them. Often this is as simple as moving house or starting at a new school, but there are other changes that can be more difficult to talk about. Like the change that happens when their parents split up or a close relative dies. Other actors in the group have often had to deal with similar problems, and when these stories are told, people realise that their own experiences and emotional responses are not uncommon.

Objects

The actors bring in an object that means something to them or has a particular significance in their lives. Then they tell the other actors why the object is important to them.

The reason that the object is so helpful is that the actors don't feel pressured to talk about themselves. They feel that they are talking about the object. It becomes the focus of their concentration and helps to remove their inhibitions. Talking about objects can often reveal difficult emotional life experiences.

Devising

The group creates a devised piece of theatre based on the things they have talked about.

The actors' stories have been told without any pressure whatsoever. Sometimes the stories have been quite funny. Sometimes the actors have talked about their best friend or a favourite teacher. Sometimes they have talked about their family life or growing up in a small village or their gap year. They have often talked about bullying or rites of passage. But once life-changing stories are shared, fears and anxieties are made public, or the experience of grief and loss is brought out into the open, then the atmosphere changes. The actors feel as if they are in a safe environment, and they can start to trust each other.

The important part of this whole project lies in telling the stories, because it is vital for actors to have the ability to tap in to their own emotional experiences. The actors can then learn how emotional experiences can be a source of power for them as creative artists.

Wallpaper

A roll of wallpaper is stretched out on the floor and the actors use coloured felt-tip pens to write or draw anything they like about themselves or what they have heard during the storytelling process.

It is important that the actors feel they can express themselves freely on the roll of wallpaper. They can respond to things that other people have written, and they can move around and write anywhere there is a blank space. This process goes on until the roll of wallpaper is full up. It then becomes a reference point for devising a piece of theatre, as certain themes and ideas emerge that are important to people in the group.

Themed Sections

The actors get into several small groups and each group chooses a theme they feel connected with in order to devise three or four minutes of theatre.

After having shared some very powerful stories during the previous sessions, the creative part of the project can now flourish, as the actors use their instincts to make innovative and entertaining theatre.

Working without supervision, the groups have to make their own decisions on how to present their particular chosen theme. For instance, they may choose to work on the theme of bullying at school, so perhaps they decide to act out short bullying scenarios. Or they may decide to use bullying phrases in a more abstract manner, or use physical movement to express their emotional reaction to bullying. The actors should be encouraged to find unexpected and interesting ways to present their theme.

All the small groups should work at the same time, and have about twenty to thirty minutes on a particular theme before they present their work to everyone else. These are like sketches. Half-formed ideas that may or may not be used later on. After each presentation there is a short group discussion about it.

The actors then divide themselves into different small groups and work on some more themes or ideas inspired by the roll of wallpaper. Sometimes the whole group can take a shared theme, like playground games or sexism, and at other times only a couple of people can work on a story that is particularly important to them. Sometimes a sensitive story can be expressed as a piece of abstract movement. Music can be used. Sometimes poetry. Dialogue can be written and performed. Dance. Moments of silence. Images. The actors create different sections that will each become part of the final presentation.

The group discuss each section and make notes about what they have seen, and gradually a complete piece of theatre begins to emerge in the group consciousness. This part of the process will take several sessions, depending on the size of the group.

Creating the Piece

The actors create a devised piece of theatre based on the stories that have been shared with the group.

Working as a whole group, the actors choose which of the devised sections will become part of the final presentation. They examine the work they have done so far and decide how to refine and improve the chosen sections and put them together in a coherent order. There are no rules for this kind of work. The group have to make their own decisions. The final piece can be themed or it can be a loosely connected series of incidents. It can be amusing at times, and poignant at others. It can be dramatic, artistic and entertaining.

This is the rehearsal part of the process and will usually take three or four sessions.

Presenting the Piece

The actors perform a piece of theatre based on their work.

Comprised of actors, the group is perfectly placed to use these stories as a piece of effective theatre. They can create a performance that will not only be entertaining, but will make members of the audience reflect on their own lives. It can be an emotional experience for both actors and audience alike.

It's usually best to do this work with a new group of actors who don't know each other very well. No cliques will have been formed and, generally speaking, it will be a level playing field. The actors will often come from very different backgrounds so the stories will broaden everyone's perception of what it is to be a human being. It is essential that actors learn to express themselves, and this whole process will help them feel free to do that, as the barriers of inhibition are gradually eroded away.

It's important that actors learn to work together, understand each other's lives and share true emotional experiences.

2
Lonelyhearts

DUKE. There is a kind of character in thy life,
That to th' observer doth thy history
Fully unfold.

Measure for Measure (1.1)

CHARACTER WORK USED TO BE ABOUT USING DIFFERENT accents, having a different way of walking and transforming your appearance with nose-putty, make-up, wigs and a padded costume. When Laurence Olivier started out in regional repertory theatre, his one big aim was to make sure that the audience didn't recognise that he was the same actor who was in last month's play. Character was a surface transformation. Something you put on. But since the age of film and television, that has changed somewhat. Character transformation has become much more subtle. As Stanislavsky said:

'Why devote so much care to the external appearance? Why not rather make up the soul?'

Nowadays, people often complain that actors are just being themselves and that they are the same in everything they do. These people would say that the age of transformation is over. But I would disagree.

It's true that actors often play characters who are very similar to themselves, but, think about it, no two people are really alike. Even identical twins each have their own personality and particular life experience. So although the exterior appearance of a character may be exactly the same as the actor who plays the part – and they may speak with the same voice, have the same physicality, and even wear the same clothes – the true transformation of the modern actor lies deep within their soul.

At ArtsEd we want our students to understand the process of internal transformation and subtle characterisation very early on in the training, and we do that without using scripts or any predetermined outline of character. We do it by showing them a process of character creation that draws on their own life experience, their observation of other people, and their ability to create and build a character experientially through improvisation. We do it with a series of exercises we call 'lonelyhearts'.

Observation

There's a story in *Zen and the Art of Motorcycle Maintenance* by Robert Pirsig where he describes an incident that happened on a creative-writing course. As I remember it, one of the students wanted to write an essay about the United States. The tutor's heart sank at the enormity of the subject, so suggested, without disparagement, that she narrow it down to just her local town. When the essay was due, the student had nothing to show. 'I tried and tried,' she said. 'But I couldn't think of anything to say.' The tutor could see that the student was frustrated. 'Okay,' he said. 'Forget the whole town. Just write about the main street.' The next day it was the same problem. No essay and a lot more frustration. By this point the tutor was starting to get frustrated himself. 'You're not looking!' he said. 'The more you *look* the more you *see*. Narrow it down to the front of one building on the main street. Start with the upper left-hand brick.'

The next day the student came back full of excitement. She handed him a five-thousand-word essay. The subject was the front of the Opera House on the main street of Bozeman,

Montana. 'I sat in the hamburger stand across the street,' she said, 'and started writing about the first brick, and the second brick, and then by the third brick it all started to come and I couldn't stop. They thought I was crazy, and they kept kidding me, but here it all is.'

It's amazing what you can actually see if you examine the details.

Observation of the Room

The actors walk around the room looking at everything.

And I mean really looking. They should start taking notice of things they usually take for granted. A bit of paintwork that is peeling away. The light fittings on the ceiling. The way the door fits into the door frame. The handle of the door. The chairs that they sit on every day. They should make a mental note of the colour, the texture, the shape and the size of all the things they look at. As they do this, they will realise how much they usually ignore. Each aspect of the room that they observe has a history. A story to tell.

Observation of a Detail

The actors choose something in the room, examine it in detail and then tell the rest of the group all about it.

As the actor focuses their attention on one particular item or part of the room, they should think about its history and purpose. Who might have put it there? What is the relevance of its position in the room? How old is it? How does it work? If it's chipped or broken, how did it get damaged? etc.

After the actors have had time to think about the item or part of the room they have been examining, each one of them should tell the rest of the group about it. They should start with the observable facts, but then they can move on to their conjecture about its history and purpose. It's amazing how much they will find that there is to say about even a simple light switch.

Observation of the World

The actors imagine that they are aliens (who look exactly like human beings) who have just landed on Earth and are seeing everything for the first time. In pairs they go out into the street, observing and discussing everything that they see.

As they walk around, the actors should describe each tree, car and paving stone, etc., to each other in great detail. They should do this for about fifteen minutes, and they should make sure that they concentrate on the objects they see and not the people.

Observation of the Self

The actors make an objective view of the way they themselves behave in different situations and with different people.

There is no doubt that we all have different ways of behaving to suit certain situations. For instance, the way someone behaves with their partner is often very different from the way they behave with their parents. It is also different from the way they behave with their peers, their colleagues or their tutors.

Over several days, the actors should make an objective observation of their own behaviour in different situations. They can start off by making a mental note of the way they talk to other people. Their choice of language when they talk with their parents isn't the same as the way they talk with their friends. They use different vocal qualities and turns of phrase. Their vocal 'mood' can also vary. While talking to some people they may be perky and bright, but others may appear disinterested and offhand.

Then they should notice the way they project their personality in different situations. For instance, they may seem more confident with their partners than they do with their fellow actors. Their posture may vary. Their physical energy may change. People do a lot of 'acting' in their everyday lives to suit the situation they are in, so the actors should start to build an objective view of their own behaviour and the various ways they present themselves.

The actors should write notes about the different ways they behave in some of the following situations:

- In a pub or bar
- In classes
- Out shopping
- With their parents
- On the phone
- With a partner
- On the Tube
- At the bank
- With their brothers and sisters
- With old school friends

Their notes should contain the following observations of their own behaviour in each of the situations they choose:

- Physical posture
- Vocal quality
- Choice of language
- Flirtatiousness
- Seriousness
- Mannerisms
- The way they project themselves
- Their sense of themselves
- How attractive they feel

Being Themselves

Each actor demonstrates to the rest of the group three different ways they behave with other people.

This can be done in a couple of ways. For instance, they could do a solo demonstration by making an imaginary phone call to their parents, and then another to an old school friend. And a third to their boyfriend or girlfriend. Or they could present an improvised conversation with other actors in the group who are pretending to be their parents or school friends, etc.

It's quite a revelation to the actors who are watching, because most of the time they only see each other behaving the way they do with the rest of the group. Tough, macho boys can be quite soppy with their girlfriends. Shy, quiet girls can be really stroppy with their parents.

Observation of Others

The actors go out into the street to observe how other people behave.

They should go to cafés, supermarkets, parks or anywhere they can watch people without being observed. They should be very careful how they do this, in case they freak someone out. It may sound invasive to observe strangers, even if the strangers don't know it's happening, but as long as the actors observe without judgement, interference or imposition, it's actually quite harmless.

Each actor finds a suitable public place to observe a stranger and then writes notes about the following things:

- Mannerisms
- Vocal qualities
- Laughter
- Posture
- Energy level
- Confidence
- How they use their hands
- The language that they use (particular words and phrases)
- The way they dress
- Status (and how it changes with different people)

Based on their observations so far, the actor uses their imagination to speculate about the life of the person they have been observing, and writes notes in answer to the following questions:

- What is their name?
- Where do they live?

- What sort of work do they do?
- Do they have a partner/family/children, etc.?
- Are they happy or sad?
- What are they looking for in life?
- What is their background?

Being Someone Else

Each actor adopts the mannerisms, speech patterns, energy levels, etc. of the person they have observed, and then the actors improvise short scenes with each other as those people.

Before they start the improvisations, the actors should get into small groups and tell each other about the people they have observed. This will help them consolidate their observations and give them confidence to take on extreme mannerisms or speech patterns.

The improvised scenes should be done in pairs and should be quite simple. For instance, the actors could be two strangers meeting at a train station, or in a shop, or a waiting room. If the scenarios are reasonably bland they won't overwhelm the character exploration.

Discussion

After all the actors have done their improvisations, the group should discuss which aspects of the observations were the most helpful, and whether the mere fact of taking on another person's behaviour and vocal patterns gives an actor a greater understanding of that person's character.

Lonelyhearts

The object of this series of exercises is to show how actors can create characters from the inside and the outside at the same time. They can combine observed mannerisms, factual knowledge and their own creative imagination to support and express the inner life of a character.

The actors also learn how to develop a complex, multilayered character by experiencing some of that character's life through improvisation. Actors often learn more by *being* their characters than they do by *talking about* them. As I said earlier, these improvisations must be truthful. No one should try to impress or entertain the people who are watching, otherwise the point of the improvisation is lost.

Perfect Partners Dating Agency

This series of exercises will culminate in a lonelyhearts link-up session, which will involve improvised meetings between lonelyhearts characters who know nothing at all about each other – so it works best if the actors have been working through the process in two entirely separate groups. For some of the following improvisations, the acting tutor can perform simple, truthful role-play improvisations to help guide the actors through the process and keep them in character. For later sessions, the acting tutor can take on the role of someone who has set up a fictitious dating agency called Perfect Partners. For the lonelyhearts link-up session it is preferable to have two acting tutors role-playing associates from Perfect Partners so that both groups can be kept apart until the last minute.

Choosing a Character

Each actor selects a character they find interesting by looking through the personal ads in newspapers or magazines.

These ads are often listed in what are known as the 'lonelyhearts columns'. Although it is possible to use the internet to find detailed descriptions of people looking for partners, it is actually best to use the simple three- or four-line newspaper or magazine postings. These concise, abbreviated entries can be quite evocative, and they leave plenty of space for the actors' creative imaginations to fly.

In London, *Time Out* is a great source for this exercise. The advertisements are paid for by the word, so, in order to save money, the people who post them often use a short-hand code, much like the abbreviations used in text messages. Here are a few of the more popular codes and their explanations:

WLTM	Would like to meet
GSOH	Good sense of humour
LTR	Long-term relationship
TLC	Tender loving care
NS	Non-smoker
BDSM	Kinky sex (bondage, discipline, sadism, masochism)
OH	Own home
OFAC	Own flat and car
SWF	Single white female
ACA	All calls answered

Euphemisms are also used, especially when people don't want to be too explicit about their desires but still need to contact other people with the same interests. For instance, 'physical relationship', 'open-minded female' and 'sensuous male' are all indications that sex is on the cards, whereas 'possible relationship' or 'long-term relationship' are more likely to indicate a desire for romance. 'Curvaceous', 'voluptuous' or 'well-built' usually means fat, and 'petite' means small. Some people don't want to brag about their wealth, so they write 'solvent', which means they are quite well off. After looking through some of these ads it's quite easy to get the picture.

Although contemporary acting often involves being a character who is close in age and background to the actor, for this exercise it is useful for the actors to broaden their range of choices by choosing people who are very unlike themselves. I suppose I could go the whole hog and say that gender is not an issue, but since girls often have to play male characters in school, and boys find it very hard to play female characters without feeling silly, I suggest that the actors choose characters of the same gender. Having said that, it would be fine to choose someone who has a different accent, a different background, or a different sexual orientation.

However, since these characters will eventually be going out into the real world, it is best if they choose someone who is within an age range that will be believable when they meet strangers.

Character Questions

Each actor writes down the answers to some of the character questions found in Chapter 5 (pages 87–90).

As the actors build their lonelyhearts characters, it is important to remember that the ads have been posted by real people who are genuine in their desire to meet other people. This is not an opportunity to be judgemental or to make fun of anyone, so the answers to the character questions should be carefully considered to ensure that they are reasonable assumptions. At this stage it is only necessary to answer the questions that might be useful.

Choosing a Character's Music

Each actor selects a piece of music that they think is appropriate for their lonelyhearts character.

Music often stimulates an emotional response and, as such, it is a useful point of focus for the actor's intuitive imagination.

The music the actors choose can either be something that they feel their lonelyhearts character would listen to themselves, or it can be a piece of music that seems to embody the life of their lonelyhearts character. As they think about their selection and listen to different pieces of music, the actors will get a deeper understanding of their lonelyhearts character's hidden life.

Writing a Character Monologue

Each actor takes on the persona of their lonelyhearts character and writes a first-person monologue based on all the information they have gathered so far.

By this time the actors will have gathered quite a lot of facts about their lonelyhearts character, some as the result of the ad, some as the result of reading between the lines of the ad, and some as a result of letting their imaginations answer questions about character. Now they can start to use their acting skills to build on these foundations.

In order to get in the right mood, the actors should take the time to think about their lonelyhearts character. They should play their selected piece of music to help them concentrate and they should gradually allow themselves to 'become' the character.

When they have done that, the actors should play their character's music while they write a first-person monologue about who they are, why they have posted a lonelyhearts ad, and what sort of person they would like to meet. They can also add any background information that they think might be helpful. Family background. Educational background. Relationship background. And so on.

This exercise is best done as homework, where the actors can play their characters' music without disturbing other people. But if the exercise is done in a rehearsal room, the actors can either wear headphones as they write their monologue, or do the exercise without playing music at all. They can write as much as they like, but somewhere between three hundred and five hundred words would be appropriate. This will probably take them about thirty minutes.

A Character File

The actors should start to collect all their written work in a file or folder for future reference.

During the course of this process, it is useful for the actors to refer back to the work they have done in the creation of their lonelyhearts character. Sometimes it will help them become their character and at other times it will simply be a reminder of things they may have forgotten.

A Significant Object

Each actor brings an object to rehearsals that they imagine has some significance for their lonelyhearts character.

In the same way that the actors brought in a significant object when they were telling stories about themselves (see Chapter 1), they should now find something they think would be important to their lonelyhearts character. The object could be an item of clothing, a favourite teddy bear, a present from someone their lonelyhearts character loves, a train ticket to London, anything. However mundane it may seem, each actor should think about the reason that this object could be important for their lonelyhearts character. If they haven't got a suitable object amongst their own possessions, a trip to a charity shop can often be a way to solve the problem.

Presenting the Character

Each actor places their lonelyhearts character's significant item in front of them, plays their character's music in the background, and reads their monologue out loud to the rest of the group in character.

Presenting their lonelyhearts characters to the rest of the group in this way will help the actors to get a close emotional connection to the character.

After each actor has presented their monologue, they come out of character and participate in a group discussion about their lonelyhearts character choices and what they have created so far. Additional ideas should be thrown into the pot by the rest of the group for further consideration by the actor. If they are found to be useful they can be added to the mix.

The significant object and the chosen piece of music will become helpful 'keys' that the actor can use to access the emotional life of their lonelyhearts character during rehearsals.

A Character Diary

From this point on, each actor creates a diary for their lonelyhearts character.

This diary should be written as if it was the lonelyhearts character's own diary. For instance, the above exercises could be written up as follows:

> 'Today I met a group of new people. I had been asked to bring a piece of music to play that I have some connection

to, so I brought _______ because _______. I was also asked to bring an object that is significant to me. I brought _______ because _______. Then I told them all about myself. Afterwards we had a discussion. It was all about me and I began to realise that _______.' (Etc.)

It's useful to put everything into words because it will become a focus for further reflection and a reminder of the things that may have been discovered during a particular session. The diary can be kept in the character file.

The Quiz Night

As their lonelyhearts characters, the actors improvise a quiz night. The quizmaster is the director or tutor who is running the session.

This session is the first opportunity for the actors, as their lonelyhearts characters, to be involved in an extended group improvisation. These group improvisations become a major part of the creative process from now on as the actors build their characters experientially.

For this session, the actors should each arrive as their lonelyhearts characters and bring something that their character might use to pass the time. A drawing book, some knitting, a book to read, perhaps an iPad or a PSP, a yo-yo or some worry beads – whatever would seem to be appropriate. If they want to wear items of clothing that will help them feel like their lonelyhearts character then they can, but at this stage it's not essential.

They are told beforehand that they are meeting for a quiz night, and they should treat the whole group improvisation as if that was the reason they have come. When they first arrive, they should talk amongst themselves as any group of strangers would who were meeting for a quiz night. Their lonelyhearts characters may be excited about the prospect of having some fun, or they may be nervous about meeting new people. They may feel confident about the prospect of a quiz, or they may feel anxious. Whatever would be appropriate for their character.

The whole session should be run like a real quiz night with the director/tutor acting as the master of ceremonies; the only difference is that the questions are really character-building questions, and the answers should just be written down rather than being discussed. The lonelyhearts characters can interact with each other at any time, in the same way that people would interact at a real quiz night.

Here is a list of questions that can be asked:

- What is your name?
- What is your date of birth?
- What sort of school did you go to?
- How well did you do at school (qualifications, etc.)?
- What is your family background?
- What is your present domestic situation?
- How do you earn money at the moment?
- How would you like to be earning money in the future?
- Who is your best friend?
- How much time do you spend with your friends?
- What do you like doing when you socialise?
- What is your favourite book?
- What is your favourite TV programme?
- What is your favourite film?
- What is your favourite piece of art?
- What is your interest in culture?
- What is your interest in politics?
- What travel destinations are you interested in?
- How do you spend your holidays?

When the quiz is over there will, of course, be no winner. But the characters can interact with each other just as they might after a real quiz night.

Naturally, the answers to the quiz questions can be added to the character file.

The Evening Class

The actors, as their lonelyhearts characters, do a group improvisation in which they have all arrived early for evening classes at an adult-education college. The improvisation takes place as they wait for their classes to start.

This exercise is designed to help the actors to start thinking in the way that their lonelyhearts character would think if they were having a conversation with strangers. They are employing Stanislavsky's 'Magic If'. In other words, they are discovering how their lonelyhearts character would behave if they were in that situation. They shouldn't pre-plan how to behave, they should just be 'in the moment'.

It's best to put the actors into groups of three or four for this exercise so that the quiet characters are not overwhelmed by the more extrovert characters.

Prior to the session, the actors are told the following:

- **They have each enrolled for an evening class in an adult-education establishment** – so they must decide what sort of class their lonelyhearts character would want to join. A language class, pottery, martial arts, painting, car maintenance, etc.
- **When the improvisation starts they must imagine that they have arrived at the adult-education establishment half an hour before the classes start** – so they should each decide why their lonelyhearts character is early. Maybe their lonelyhearts character made a mistake about the time, or maybe they are always early. Maybe they don't have a watch. Maybe they didn't have time to go home before the class so they came straight from work. Whatever the reason, each actor should know exactly why their lonelyhearts character is early.
- **Each actor, as their lonelyhearts character, must talk to the other people who are waiting, even if their character is shy** – it's important that they find a reason for their lonelyhearts character to talk, otherwise they won't discover anything new. Their characters have already posted their

lonelyhearts ads, so they could be using this evening class as another way to meet new people.

- **They must stay in character for the whole discussion and sustain any physical, vocal or emotional mannerisms that they may have discovered so far.**
- **They must neither dominate the conversation nor avoid it. They should talk and listen and try to learn as much about their lonelyhearts character as they can.**

This improvisation should continue for about thirty minutes. When it's over, each actor writes their lonelyhearts character's diaries about the experience while it's still fresh in their minds.

As always, this exercise should be followed by a discussion with the whole group about the experience and what they might have discovered.

The Self-help Group

The actors get into groups of six or seven and, taking one lonelyhearts character at a time, they improvise a series of self-help sessions. Each improvisation lasts about ten minutes.

For this exercise, each of the actors has to imagine what sort of self-help group their lonelyhearts characters might attend and why they would attend it. The following list of problems and possibilities can be a helpful guide:

- Alcohol dependency
- Addiction – drugs, cigarettes, chocolate, trashy magazines, the internet, etc.
- Lack of confidence
- Depression
- Anxiety
- Anger management
- Obsessive Compulsive Disorder
- Eating disorders – anorexia, bulimia, overeating
- Agoraphobia

- Claustrophobia
- Inability to make commitments
- Fear of flying/spiders/snakes, etc.

The actor going first tells the rest of the group what sort of self-help session they feel their lonelyhearts character would attend and then leaves the room to prepare. The rest of the group take a minute or two to create characters who they think might go to such a session. These should be different from their own lonelyhearts characters.

The lonelyhearts character then comes back into the room and the improvisation starts. The lonelyhearts character should do most of the talking in order to delve into their own particular problems. The rest of the group can keep the improvisation going by asking questions and talking briefly about their made-up characters' own experiences.

This is followed by a group discussion before the next actor has their turn.

This exercise helps the actors to think more deeply about the emotional life of their lonelyhearts character. The rest of the group help out by being involved and supportive, making it possible for the lonelyhearts character to open themselves up in a way that may not normally be possible for them.

The Perfect Partners Questionnaire

Each actor, as their lonelyhearts character, fills in the questionnaire below.

Completing the questionnaire is to prepare the lonelyhearts characters for a meeting with a representative from the Perfect Partners dating agency. This questionnaire can be completed by the actors at home, or as part of a group session with each actor working on their own. It should take about twenty to thirty minutes.

Perfect Partners

Please fill in the questionnaire and then hand it in to your representative at the beginning of the interview.

Please complete all sections below.

What are you seeking?

Close friendship ☐
Marriage ☐
Long-term relationship ☐
Fun and laughter ☐

What are your interests?

....
....
....

What leisure activities do you partake in?

....
....
....

What encouraged you to come to a dating agency?

....
....
....

A little about the person you would like to meet:

....
....
....

What age range would you prefer to meet?

From...... To...... No preference ☐

What height range would you prefer to meet?

From...... To...... No preference ☐

Would you mind if they had children?

Yes ☐ No ☐ No preference ☐

Do you mind if they smoke?

Yes ☐ No ☐ No preference ☐

What educational background would you prefer?

GCSE/A-Levels	☐	Degree	☐
PhD	☐	No preference	☐

What interests and pastimes would you prefer?
(Please tick between one and four boxes.)

Fine art	☐	Science	☐
Music	☐	Dance	☐
Theatre	☐	Cinema	☐
Printed media	☐	Holidays	☐
Outdoor activities	☐	Literature	☐
Sports	☐	Pets	☐
Gardening	☐	Interior design	☐
Cooking	☐	Conversation	☐

Any additional information that may be relevant:

....
....
....
....
....
....
....
....
....

The Perfect Partners Interview

Each actor has a one-to-one interview with a representative from the Perfect Partners Dating Agency.

This interview itself is as much like a dating-agency interview as possible. The acting tutor role-plays a representative from the agency, and the improvisation is simply to find out as much as possible about the lonelyhearts character.

Before the improvisation starts, the actors should dress in the clothes their lonelyhearts characters would wear. They should also think about their characters' hopes and expectations, so they will be able to discuss these things. The actors should be in character before, during and after the interview.

While they are waiting for the interview to start, the actors, as their lonelyhearts characters, should fill in their diaries. They should write about their character's emotional state as they embark on this journey into the unknown. They should also make another entry in their diaries after they have had the interview so they can express how their lonelyhearts character is feeling while it is still fresh in their minds.

Although the tutor can behave much like themselves, it is important that they have a clear idea of their own invented character and that they take the role-play seriously. They should use a different name, invent a history for Perfect Partners and, if there is more than one tutor involved, they should know a bit about each other and their roles within the agency.

To make this as realistic as possible the tutor should also dress appropriately and arrange the rehearsal room so that it looks something like an office. The more realistic everything seems, the easier it is for the actors to find the truth of the improvisation.

Each of the lonelyhearts characters can be given a sheet with testimonials from satisfied clients:

Perfect Partners

Testimonials from Satisfied Clients

'I'm pleased to inform you that I have a new lady in my life. Thank you for the excellent service provided.' *Mr D, Warwickshire*

'I just had to let you know I was very impressed with the way in which the interview was carried out. Chrissie really was great and made me feel very comfortable. Many of the questions she asked were very thought provoking!! She was very professional but friendly.' *Miss G, Dorset*

'He was a great match! He's intelligent, sporty, well-travelled and attractive. We had a lot in common and I am very impressed with the matching! I was certainly attracted to him and I think the feeling was mutual. I hope we meet again!' *Anna, Swiss Cottage*

'B was a lovely man – we had a great date and we exchanged numbers. He restored my faith in decent men!' *Marianne, London*

'K is extremely charming, personable and good company. A great first date!' *Charlotte, Windsor*

'Thank you all so much for matching J and I – you got it spot on this time! He is the best thing that has ever happened to me! I thought it would be nice to send you an update on how things are going with us. To say they are great is, I suppose, a bit of an understatement. We have just found out that we are going to be parents in February and are both thrilled to bits by the news. From singletons to parents in less than a year, but I guess when you meet the right one there's no point in hanging around!' *Elaine, London*

'He really made me laugh and came across as genuine and down-to-earth. We had plenty in common to talk about and are planning to see one another again!' *Helen, Berkshire*

'A lovely man and a real gentleman. We enjoyed lively, intelligent conversation and found lots of things in common. It was a delight to spend the evening with him. Thank you so much for introducing us.' *Sarah, London*

'R was chatty and amiable. We lost track of time and were the last ones out of the restaurant. A good sign!' *Peter, Richmond*

'It seems extraordinary but S has completely won me over. I don't know how we were matched but it works! A thousand thanks to Perfect Partners. I am very happy!' *John, South Kensington*

The tutor, as the Perfect Partners representative, should have a selection of questions to get the ball rolling:

- Did you have a good journey?
- Did you find us okay?
- How did you hear about Perfect Partners?
- Are you interested in meeting a man or a woman?
- Do you have any pet hates?
- Do you think looks are important?
- What is your idea of a perfect evening?

The tutor can then continue the interview by using the lonelyhearts character's questionnaire as a stimulus for further discussion.

At the end of the interview the Perfect Partners representative should tell the lonelyhearts character that they will soon be given details of a prospective partner and that a meeting will be arranged.

After the interviews are over, all the actors should come out of character and have a group discussion about the things they discovered.

Going Out in Character

The actors, as their lonelyhearts characters, go out into the street and interact with the people they meet.

As I have mentioned, it could be considered intrusive to improvise with members of the public, but if the lonelyhearts characters and the conversations are realistic then the people they talk to will have no idea that they are involved in an acting exercise, and no harm is done.

This will be the first time the actors go out into the real world in character, and it will help them to have specific tasks to perform, such as asking a stranger the way to the station, or deciding which shop their character would like best. They could also engage a shop assistant in a conversation about something their character might like to buy.

The actors learn a lot by doing this exercise. It's extremely liberating to discover that complete strangers will think their invented characters are real. It makes them realise that quite extreme characterisations can be readily accepted. This is important because actors should understand that being cautious is boring. As long as their creative decisions are supported by an inner truth, their characterisations can be really bold. Anyway, they will know if they are being phoney when they are improvising with strangers, because they will feel phoney as they do it.

There is no way of knowing how members of the public are going to behave and this exercise is quite daunting for the actors, so for their sake and for the sake of the people they meet, they should be asked to observe a few safety rules:

- When they are interacting with the general public, they should try to think in character.
- They shouldn't use their phone, or give their phone number to a stranger.
- They shouldn't drink coffee if they don't normally.
- They shouldn't drink any alcohol.
- They shouldn't smoke cigarettes if they don't normally.

- They shouldn't feel the need to buy anything they can't easily afford.
- They shouldn't go to the hairdresser/dentists/opticians, etc.
- They shouldn't sign up to pay by direct debit to a charity.
- They shouldn't get involved in anything they wouldn't want to follow through.
- They shouldn't get into arguments with strangers.
- If they find themselves in a difficult or dangerous situation, they should come out of character immediately.

The Solo Date

A representative of Perfect Partners sends the lonelyhearts characters out into the street to meet someone for a 'date'.

For this exercise, the actors dress as their lonelyhearts characters and arrive for the session as if they were they were arriving at the Perfect Partners office. They are met by the tutor who is role-playing a representative of the agency. The actors should remain in character for the whole session, only coming out of character when they are told to by the tutor.

The lonelyhearts characters are each given the details of a meeting that has been arranged for them. They are given the name of their prospective partner, his or her age, and a specific location. This may be in a café, outside a particular shop, or at some other identifiable place. Cafés are best because the lonelyhearts characters can sit and have a tea or coffee while they wait. They should take their diaries with them and write about how they are feeling as they wait for their date to arrive.

Whether or not they actually meet their date, they are told to be back at Perfect Partners (the rehearsal room) by a certain time, usually about three-quarters of an hour after they leave. As before, they should interact with the general public as long as they are sensible and careful.

Although they don't know it, this date is a bit of a trick because no one is going to meet them, and they will just have to sit and wait. But as they do that they will be inclined to think about their situation and that will give them the opportunity to write in their diaries.

When the actors return to Perfect Partners, they stay in character and continue the improvisation with the tutor who is still role-playing a Perfect Partners representative. The lonelyhearts characters may well be quite annoyed that no one has turned up for the date and the Perfect Partners representative has to deal with it.

Before the end of the session, the actors are told to come out of character and a group discussion follows about the whole experience.

Going Out in Pairs

Each lonelyhearts character goes out into the street to meet up with another lonelyhearts character as if they were friends.

At the start of this session the actors get together in character pairs that have something in common. During the previous improvisations each lonelyhearts character will usually have met another character in the group that they get on with.

Before they go out into the street, the actors arrange to meet up at a particular time and place. They should give themselves enough time to get there comfortably. Usually about fifteen to twenty minutes. They should then take a minute or two to get into character before they set off separately for the meeting.

They should do some of the following things before they meet up:

- Go to a bookshop and think about what books their lonelyhearts character might read.
- Go to a supermarket and decide what their lonelyhearts characters might want to eat that evening. Thinking about whether they would cook for themselves, buy a ready meal or go out to a restaurant.
- Go to a clothes shop and look at the clothes their lonelyhearts character might want to buy to go out on a date.
- Talk to strangers whenever possible.

- Have opinions about the various things they pass on the way: churches, pubs, factories, health-food shops, butcher's, statues, police officers, homeless people, etc.
- Walk through the park and think about the countryside.

When they eventually meet up, the two lonelyhearts characters should discuss some of their opinions with each other. They should also each talk about their lonelyhearts characters' home life. In fact, because they are friends, they can have quite deep conversations about life, relationships, hopes, regrets, etc.

When it is time to finish, they should say goodbye and make their way back to the rehearsal room separately.

As usual, this improvisation should be followed by a group discussion and then the actors, as their lonelyhearts characters, should have the opportunity to write in their diaries about the experience.

Lonelyhearts Link-up

Meetings are arranged between lonelyhearts characters who have never met, and they are sent on a 'date' by representatives of Perfect Partners.

For this final session, which takes half a day, each lonelyhearts character has two 'dates' with two other lonelyhearts characters. If they have been working in separate groups, then the meeting will be between lonelyhearts characters who are entirely unknown to each other. It is ideal to have two tutors role-playing representatives of Perfect Partners: one tutor in charge of each group.

Tutors' Preparation

Before the lonelyhearts link-up session, the tutors make a list of meetings across the two groups, pairing up characters who seem to be appropriate for each other. This can be quite tricky, so in order to make it fair, each lonelyhearts character is given two meetings during the session, one of which might not be quite as suitable as the other. Perfect Partners can be blamed for any poor pairings; after all, the actors will all have experienced a previous lonelyhearts link-up when they were sent on a date and no one turned up!

The tutors also plan out where each couple will meet and prepare a map of the area with the meeting places clearly marked. This is to ensure that there are no mistakes.

Two rehearsal rooms should be prepared as if they were rooms hired by Perfect Partners.

(It's important to tell everyone in the building, particularly the doorman, that the actors will be in character and that they might appear to be behaving strangely!)

Actors' Preparation

This exercise starts the evening before the session, when the actors read through their lonelyhearts diary before they go to bed. They should tell the people they live with that they are going to be in character next morning as soon as they wake up, and that no one should talk to them, or try to communicate with them unless there is a real emergency.

When they wake up on the morning of the lonelyhearts link-up, the actors should immediately get into character. They should get up, get dressed, have breakfast, and travel to the Perfect Partners office (i.e. the rehearsal rooms) as their lonelyhearts characters, so they arrive for the session fully in character. Each group will have been told to go to a specific rehearsal room.

The Date

As the lonelyhearts characters start to arrive, the tutors role-play Perfect Partners representatives and meet them at the door. Each group is sent to a different rehearsal room to keep them apart. At ArtsEd the tutors usually film this session, telling the lonelyhearts characters that we are making a record for the Perfect Partners archives.

As the lonelyhearts characters arrive at their particular rehearsal rooms, they are encouraged to chat with each other while they wait for everyone else to arrive. They will be with the same group of actors that they have been working with previously, so their lonelyhearts characters will have met each other before. They will have a shared history like the evening class, the quiz night and going out in pairs, so they will already have something to talk about.

When everyone has arrived, each lonelyhearts character is given two dates, one within the next quarter of an hour, and the other about halfway through the session. They are also given a map of the area with the location of their date clearly marked. They are asked to make sure that they are not late for the second meeting and the lonelyhearts characters from both groups are told to meet back in the same rehearsal rooms at a time which is about three-quarters of an hour before the end of the session.

And off they go.

During the session, the tutors should wander around the streets seeing how everyone is getting on. It's quite all right for the tutors to talk to any of the lonelyhearts characters they meet as long as they stay in character as the Perfect Partners representatives.

At the allotted time the lonelyhearts characters start to return. Some will be on their own and others will be in couples. Maybe some characters will be holding hands. Others may be carrying flowers. Still in character, they are encouraged to talk about the experience with each other and to meet characters from the other group whom they have never met.

When all the lonelyhearts characters have returned, they continue to chat with each other for ten minutes or so. Then the Perfect Partners representatives ask them to sit in a circle and they encourage each character to tell the rest of the group how they got on. Some will have formed very positive relationships and are already planning to meet up later; some will have become reasonably friendly with each other, but don't want to have a serious relationship; while others will have had a very disappointing time because they didn't gel with either of the people they met. None of this matters, of course, because whatever has happened, they have all experienced an extended group improvisation where they had to stay in role as a thoroughly prepared character.

Before the end of the session, one of the tutors stands up and says: 'I will count down from three and then you can all come out of character… Three… two… One! Out of character!' At this point the room will explode with excited energy and noise. It's like a cork being released from a bottle of champagne. The actors have had to concentrate on being in character since the moment they got up – and it's very demanding. There will be so much energy in the room at this point that it's impossible to get the actors to settle down to a group discussion. The tutors can go around talking to small groups or individuals. Everyone will want to talk about the experience, and it's all massively positive.

Debrief

At a later date, the actors have a group discussion about the whole experience. Spending half a day improvising in character is an exhausting business and the actors need some time to wind down and relax, so the group discussion needs to take place on another day.

The actors talk about the ups and downs of the lonelyhearts link-up, what they have learned, and how they can carry this sort of work forward when they are preparing a role in a scripted play or film. The whole process is a great boost to the actors' confidence and self-belief, because the creative work was all theirs, and the truth behind their characters stood the test of public scrutiny and a dangerous plunge into unknown territory.

This empowers the actors.

There are many variations to the creative processes employed by film and theatre directors, so actors should be encouraged to have a positive and open attitude to anything that a director may ask them to do. Of course, many theatre directors have their own rehearsal techniques and often don't use improvisation at all. And film and television rehearsals can be non-existent, with the actors being expected to arrive on the set thoroughly prepared before the filming starts.

But there are various elements of the lonelyhearts process that can be used outside the rehearsal room, either as solo work or with other actors who are keen to carry out these extended improvisations. Actors who have experienced this sort of work often get together in character when they are working on a play or preparing to film. Sometimes two of them will arrange to have dinner together in character. Sometimes a group of actors will go out to a club and stay in character for a whole evening. Usually it's not difficult for the actors to think of an extended improvisation that will be appropriate for the play or film that they are preparing.

These self-organised rehearsal improvisations can be extremely useful. After all, the more that an actor can experience the life of their character, the more they are able to present a true version of that character in performance.

And the truth is a very valuable tool when you are trying to convey a complex story with depth and detail.

3
The Text

HAMLET. The play's the thing...

Hamlet (2.2)

IN ORDER TO 'PUT ON A SHOW', 'MOUNT A PRODUCTION', 'stage a play', or whatever you want to call it, you have to start with a few ingredients. And unless you are mounting Samuel Beckett's twenty-five-second play *Breath*, which consists only of a stage 'littered with miscellaneous rubbish' and various recorded sound effects, the essential ingredient would have to be *actors*. Performers. People to do the show.

The next most important ingredient – and this will put some people's noses out of joint, particularly directors – is a *script*. Of course, you could be creating a piece of work from scratch through collaboration and improvisation, but even then you will end up with a script of some sort.

The third important ingredient, of course, is a *director* to bring it all together and make it work. Later on you will need stage managers, designers, wardrobe people, set-builders, lighting designers, a theatre, an audience and favourable reviews. And if you're making a film, you'll need all this plus an army of technicians and a load of money. But actually, an actor can start working on a script without any of these things.

And that's where we'll start. The actor and a text.

First Impressions

'What do you read, my lord?' asks Polonius (*Hamlet*, 2.2). 'Words, words, words,' Hamlet replies. Of course, it wasn't the answer that Polonius was expecting, but it couldn't be denied. When you're reading something, all you've got is words. But the difference between the words in the telephone directory and the words in a piece of literature or a newspaper article is the way the words are put together. A telephone directory doesn't really stimulate the reader's imagination. Hamlet was speaking the truth, but he was being purposely obstructive. What Polonius really wanted to know was what Hamlet was reading *about*. The substance. The content. What the words were telling Hamlet.

And words tell us a lot. Especially when they are put together in sentences. Even more when they are part of a dialogue, because then they start to bounce off each other.

For the moment, I'm going to focus on the analysis of a play script rather than a film script because I want to show how much can be learned from the dialogue. Film is a more visual medium. It uses pictures to tell the story, so film scripts tend to have more visual descriptions than dialogue. However, a lot of the following analysis can be helpful for an actor working on a film script, especially as they unravel the details of a character.

Most playwrights will have a very clear vision of how their play will look onstage as they write it. Their imagination visualises everything: the characters; the way people move about the stage; the environment of the play; the way the characters talk; the characters' emotions; and the effect the whole thing will have on an audience. And that whole imaginary world that exists in the playwright's head is condensed and refined into the things the characters say to each other. The dialogue. Playwrights carefully choose the right words and the appropriate sentence construction in order to convey character, relationships, emotion, plot, action, in fact the whole caboodle. It's all in the dialogue. Generally speaking, that is what a play is: the words that the characters speak.

And that's where we'll start.

Reading a play for the first time is quite a tricky business for anyone. It's so easy to get mixed up with the character's names and forget who has done what. And there are very few descriptive passages to keep the reader on track because the playwright knows that the audience will eventually connect with the way the actors present the play. In fact, reading a play for the first time is so tricky there are even books about how to do it. My advice is to read a play slowly, try to visualise the characters, and make notes as you go along.

Reading the Play

The first reading of a play should be approached as objectively as possible.

When actors read a play for the first time, they experience the plot unfolding without any preconceptions of where it will all end. The characters are revealed bit by bit, and the climaxes and changes of rhythm are surprising and unexpected. This first reading is the closest that actors get to the way an audience will eventually experience the play. As the actors discover more and more detail during rehearsals, the less they will remember this initial overall effect. They won't be able to see the wood for the trees, as they say.

If an actor has been cast in a specific role, it's even harder to read the play objectively. The actor will tend to see things entirely from the perspective of their character, and they will often focus solely on his or her shifting emotions as they read. They will sometimes even try out bits of characterisation and experiment with they way their character might talk. But this is far too early because it might lead them to make stereotypical, one-dimensional or even wrong-headed decisions.

So, if it's at all possible, I would recommend that actors read the play without knowing which character they will be playing. It's reasonably easy to make this happen in colleges and drama schools, but it's not so simple professionally, because actors will want to know which part they are playing before they accept the job. If an actor already knows the casting, I would recommend that they try to keep an open mind, read the play as objectively as possible and focus on the overall plot. There will be plenty of time to experiment with characterisations during the rehearsal period.

Making Notes

As a script is examined and analysed, notes should be taken of any discoveries.

It may seem a rather labour-intensive way of working on a script, but if the actor has a written record of everything they have discovered about the play – the characters, the relationships, the plot, etc. – then they will be able to refer back to it later in rehearsals. Initial discoveries can easily be forgotten and then ignored. Sometimes the most basic 'truths' will become obscured by imaginative work later on in rehearsals. I've seen performances where the actor has created such an original interpretation of a character that the fundamental essence of the character has been totally lost and the play has been damaged. Polonius (Ophelia's father in *Hamlet*) may seem like a doddering old fool, but he gives his son, Laertes, the greatest advice that a father could give a son in the speech that ends: 'to thine own self be true…' This is not the advice of a fool. His position in court is also akin to a Prime Minister, and although several Prime Ministers in recent history have seemed like doddering old fools, it must be acknowledged that they were probably highly intelligent men. If an actor ignores the depth of Polonius's perception and just plays the doddering old fool, then there is no point in Hamlet verbally sparring with him as he does on several occasions.

So… everything should be written down because it is so easy to forget the basics, as more and more subtleties of interpretation are added to the mix.

The Overall Shape of the Play

After reading a play for the first time, the actors should immediately make a note of their first impressions before they forget them.

This initial analysis should contain answers to the following questions:

- **What was the playwright trying to achieve?**

  This should be a broad description of the effect that the play will have on the audience. Will it make them laugh? Will it make them cry? Will it make them think about injustice, or bravery? Is it to shock, or is it to intrigue? What is the play for and how does the plot unfold to achieve the desired effect?

- **What is the main theme of the play?**

  The main theme of a play is important because it is often the driving force of the plot. It could be about a particular aspect of the human condition, such as loneliness, or it could be an in-depth exploration of romance. It could concentrate on the destructive nature of jealousy, like Shakespeare's *Othello*, or it could be a play about infidelity, such as *Betrayal* by Harold Pinter. Maybe the play has a political theme or a pastoral theme. Maybe its theme is resilience under pressure, or the joy of life.

- **What is the plot?**

  This is simply an outline of how the plot unfolds, section by section, scene by scene.

- **Where are the climaxes within the play?**

  It's important to know the rhythm of a play. The moments when the audience will be on the edge of their seats and the times they will be able to relax. The sections where the play drives forward to some sort of climax, and the transition from that moment to the next. By pinpointing the climaxes of a play, each actor will understand their character's responsibility to the story or to the theme of the whole play.

- **Which are the most memorable scenes?**

  The scenes that stand out on first reading will be the scenes that stand out for the audience. These are important mileposts and should be noted; otherwise the balance of the play could be upset during rehearsals as the wrong scenes are given precedence.

- **Which characters are the most interesting?**

  For the actor playing the maid with only a few lines, the maid may be the most interesting character, but in order to present the play coherently the characterisation of the maid shouldn't upset the playwright's intentions. And this goes across the board. Claudius, Ophelia, Polonius, Gertrude. They're all fabulously interesting characters, but I think most people would agree that the play is ultimately about Hamlet. On first reading a play, some characters will appear to be more interesting than others. Note should be taken of who they are and why they were interesting, in order to keep an objective view of the playwright's intentions.

- **What are the relationships of the main characters in the play?**

  Character, plot and relationships. These are the substance of drama and there will be a lot of work in rehearsal to unravel and clarify all these things. But it is important to write down the relationships between the characters as they appeared on first reading.

- **What are the problems with the play?**

  Note should be taken of the sections where the plot is engaging and the sections where it drifts. Sometimes bits of the plot are unclear, and this could be solved through character and presentation. Not all plays are perfect, but they can always be improved and clarified by the way the actors decide to play the scenes.

Undisputed Facts

Having gained an overall impression of the play, it is now time to consider the undisputed facts within the text, so they can be used as foundations for the creative process. Sometimes the explorative nature of rehearsals can obscure these facts. I remember working with a very intense actor who was extremely thorough in his preparation and would never let a moment go by without questioning everything about his character's psychology and motivations. In the middle of a rehearsal, as he was trying to come to terms with a complicated speech, he screamed out with frustration: 'But how does my character know all these things?' The director, who was sympathetic to the frustrations of one of his favourite actors, stayed calm. He raised his eyebrows, opened the palms of his hands and said, slightly apologetically: 'Well, he's just read them in the letter you are holding in your left hand!'

Sometimes the facts can be more revealing than extensive psychological analysis.

The Given Circumstances

During the second reading of a play, the actors should write down all the undisputed facts or the 'given circumstances'.

Sometimes these facts will become areas of research and exploration, and sometimes they will be simple reminders for future reference.

I should make it clear right from the start that the following investigations are to identify the *writer's intentions*. It may be that the director has decided that the best way to illuminate and clarify the play is to set it in a time, place or cultural environment that is quite different from the one that the writer had in mind. I'll talk about that later on, but for now it's important to extract as much information as possible from the text itself.

- **In which era does the play take place?**

  Obviously this is of major importance and will sometimes need a large amount of research. There are certain aspects of human nature that are universal and will apply to any time and place. Macbeth's ambition. Othello's jealousy. Romeo and Juliet's teenage passion for each other. All these have their parallels today and would be easily recognised by audiences from any period of history. But Shakespeare's plays were first performed in another era, and the political climate, the racial attitudes and the cultural expectations of that particular era would have had an impact on how the characters behaved. Similarly, a play that is set in the nineteenth century will present a culture that is very different from our own. So would a play set as recently as 1969. Cultural values are continually changing and they will have a strong impact on the way the characters relate to each other.

- **Where is the play set?**

  The country, state or town where the action takes place will also have a marked effect on the attitudes and actions of the characters. The late-nineteenth-century Russia of Chekhov's plays would have been entirely different from the mid-twentieth-century docklands of Brooklyn where Arthur Miller sets *A View from the Bridge*. Later on, a certain amount of research will flesh out the basic facts, but *The Cherry Orchard* takes place in rural Russia. Full stop. It can't be ignored. The characters in *A View from the Bridge* live and work in Brooklyn. Check it out. Write it down.

- **Where does each scene take place?**

  Is the setting of a particular scene indoors or outside? Are the characters wandering through open fields or in the kitchen of a crumbling mansion? Sometimes a scene takes place in a private place and sometimes the characters are surrounded by noisy, nosey crowds. All these things affect the way people behave. If the environment is particularly important, the writer will often describe it in great detail.

- **At what time of year is each scene set?**

  The bleak midwinter affects not only the clothes that people wear, but the way that they think and behave. The lazy, hazy days of summer have a quite different quality from the grim and gloomy days of winter. Compare the films of Ingmar Bergman, made in Sweden, with the films of Pedro Almodóvar, which are set in Spain. Different personalities, to be sure, but don't you just feel that the long, dark winters will have affected Bergman differently from the bright summer sun of Almodóvar? It certainly looks like it in their films.

- **At what time of day is each scene set?**

  Do I need to explain? Mornings are different from evenings. Lunch is different from tea. The time of day affects us all.

- **What is the weather like for each scene?**

  The weather can also affect the way the characters think and behave. Writers often include weather conditions that reflect the mood of a scene.

- **What are the actual relationships of all the characters?**

  Laertes and Ophelia are brother and sister. Gertrude is Hamlet's mother. These are obvious. But sometimes relationships pass you by. If Gertrude is Hamlet's mother and Ophelia was once his girlfriend, then Gertrude was, at one time, Ophelia's prospective mother-in-law. This will bring an extra edge to how Gertrude feels when Ophelia goes mad.

- **Is there anything else?**

  There will be much more information to be gleaned from the script. On closer examination, other undisputed facts will be revealed. Remember, these should not be suppositions or speculations; they should be facts that are supported by the text. Actors should write them down because they will be useful later in rehearsals.

A Detailed Examination of Character

So now it's time to start the long and fascinating creation of character. The subtleties and complexities of trying to get to the heart of a person who only exists as words on a printed page is an intriguing business. Fun too. A lot of information about the characters can be discovered in the things that they say to each other, and the way they say them. So, having got an overall view of the structure and purpose of the play, and then having identified some of the given circumstances, it is time to start a much closer examination of the text to find out as much as possible about the individual characters.

A Character's Function in the Play

Each actor should ask themselves the following questions about their character in relation to the play as a whole:

- **What happens to my character during the play?**

  Some characters make quite complex and unexpected journeys through the course of a play. These journeys can be emotional, spiritual, romantic, adventurous, disastrous, or anything you can imagine. Sometimes things go well and sometimes they go badly. Each actor should examine what happens to their character scene by scene, and write it down. Sometimes there are major changes of direction within a scene and these too should be noted. A character's progression through a play from the beginning to the end is sometimes referred to as the character's arc.

- **What is the most important scene for my character?**

  Some scenes are pivotal moments in a character's journey. Other scenes are simply developments of plot. Actors should write down the scenes that seem to be 'milepost moments' for their character.

- **What is my character's function in the play?**

  When the playwright constructed these two hours (or so) of dramatic action, characters were invented to support and develop the themes. Each actor should ask themselves why their character is even in the play. What did the playwright have in mind when the character became part of the plot? Does the character's arc reinforce or counteract the main theme of the play? Does it drive the plot forward or does it give the audience a moment of respite? If each actor understands their character's function in the play, they will be able to support the themes and participate in the development and presentation of the play as a whole.

Basic Facts About a Character

Each actor should write a list of undisputed facts about their character that they have found in the text.

Some of these facts may already have been noted during the first reading of the play, but even so, each actor should focus on the given circumstances of their own particular character and write a comprehensive list of facts.

These facts could be found in their character's own dialogue or the things that other characters say about their character. They can also be found in the stage directions. But they should be undisputed facts, not opinions, speculations or assumptions.

- Name
- Age
- Job
- Education
- Marital status
- Ethnicity
- Etc.

Dialogue Lists

Each actor should write down specific lines of dialogue that reveal something about their character.

There is a lot of 'hidden' information in a play that can be discovered by examining the things that the characters say and the way that they say them. Actors should read the play carefully and pick out these clues with meticulous attention to detail, making lists of specific lines of dialogue. Sometimes a character tells lies, sometimes their information is inaccurate and sometimes their opinions are biased, but a clearer picture will be revealed when these lines of dialogue are isolated from the play as a whole. These lists should not be comprised of suppositions; they should be the actual words that the characters say. For example, if a character says, 'That's a nice cat,' the actor shouldn't write, 'My character seems to like cats'; they should write exactly what their character says: 'That's a nice cat.'

Each actor should write three separate lists under the following headings. Once the lists have been made they can be properly analysed:

- **Everything my character says about him or herself.**

  A lot can be learned from the things that characters say about themselves, so these lists should be thorough. For instance, when the character of Olga in Chekhov's *Three Sisters* (translation by Michael Frayn) is talking about her father's funeral, she says, 'I remember the band playing and the firing at the cemetery as they carried the coffin,' and that obviously would go on the list. But she goes on to say, 'It is warm today, we can have the windows open,' and that should also be on the list because she is saying something about herself. She feels warm. This may appear to be a line about the weather, but if further lines reveal that the character talks about the heat several times during the play and no one else mentions it, then it becomes clear that Olga is particularly affected by the temperature for some reason. Maybe she is ill. Maybe she is wearing too many clothes. Maybe the social atmosphere in the room is oppressive for her. Or perhaps she just has a marked interest in the weather.

- **Everything my character says about any of the other characters in the play.**

  An actor needs to know exactly how their character feels about all the other characters in the play, and that will be revealed in the things they say about them. This list will not only help the actor understand how his or her character treats each of the other characters individually, it will give a broader picture of their character's general attitude to other people.

- **Everything other characters say about my character.**

  This list will help the actor understand how his or her character comes across to other people. Their character may seem reasonable and charming, but if other people keep referring to how irritating they are, then the actor has to find something in their performance to create that irritation, even if it doesn't appear in the actual dialogue.

List Analysis

Having extracted as much 'hidden' information as possible, it can now be examined and analysed.

Unlike the undisputed facts and given circumstances that were gathered previously, these dialogue lists contain information that is open to interpretation. The actors now have the opportunity to draw conclusions that fit the evidence. They can make creative choices based on the clues they find in the dialogue lists. For instance, to continue the analysis of Olga's dialogue in *Three Sisters*, she says two apparently contradictory statements: 'I have felt my... youth oozing away from me every day,' and a little later: 'I feel younger than yesterday.' The actress playing Olga would have to ask herself which of these is the truth about Olga? On the other hand, if Olga's line in Act Three – 'I've aged ten years tonight' – is put on the list together with lines from her closing speech in Act Four – 'The years will pass, and we shall all be gone for good and quite forgotten' and '... if we wait a little longer, we shall find out why we live, why we suffer... Oh, if we only knew, if we only knew!' – the actress may conclude that Olga's continual reference to the passing of time is not about the loss of youth, but about the meaninglessness of life itself. By considering all these lines, the actress will have to make a choice and that choice will affect the subtext.

Each actor should write answers to the following questions about their character:

- **What are my character's attitudes and beliefs?**

  A character's likes and dislikes should be considered. Sometimes fundamental beliefs or philosophies will be uncovered that weren't apparent on first reading. As I said, these conclusions can be the result of the actor's creative imagination as long as they are supported by clues in the text.

- **How does my character feel about him or herself?**

  The way that a character speaks about him or herself is just as revealing as the things they actually say. For instance: 'I'm really happy' is obviously different from 'I'm quite happy'; but also 'I'm quite happy really' is also different from 'I'm really quite happy.' Sometimes these differences aren't spotted and the lines are learnt incorrectly. When that happens, an actor can end up creating a character that is subtly but crucially different from the one that was originally visualised by the writer, and that can upset the whole structure and purpose of the script.

- **What words or phrases are repeated by my character?**

  Without examining these lists it is easy to miss some really obvious aspects of character. Particular words or phrases may be used several times during the course of the play. For instance, if a character regularly uses words and phrases like 'I don't know' or 'maybe', it could indicate that they are unsure about expressing their opinion of things. If their lines often end with 'do you see what I mean?', it could indicate that the character is uncertain about their ability to communicate their thoughts. Repeated phrases often go unnoticed until they become part of a list.

- **What does my character say about each of the other characters?**

  Plays are often about relationships, and so a large part of the rehearsal process will be about building and understanding the dynamics of these relationships. This analysis is a good starting point for this particular exploration. The list could reveal that the character seems to be in love with several people at the same time, or that a character is ambitious or needy or arrogant. But it could reveal that people make the character feel paranoid or isolated.

- **What attitude does my character have to each of the other characters?**

  Actors should never be afraid of gut feelings and intuition, so any ideas the lists have brought to mind should be written down for consideration. They can always be altered later in rehearsals if they don't seem to fit.

- **What are the most common words or phrases that other characters use about my character?**

  When several people say similar things about a character, then it has to be assumed that their comments have some validity. This list helps to build a picture of the character from another perspective, as opinions are reinforced layer by layer. It also reveals subtle indications of character that may have been missed.

The text is a gold mine for an actor. Words on a page, carefully studied, can yield creative riches that will enhance a characterisation and make it unique and fascinating. The big danger for an actor is to make generalised assumptions and create easy-option characters. Naturally, an actor's own life experiences and characteristics should be used as part of the creative process; but without a close examination of the text, actors will tend to dilute the strongly imagined characters that the writer may have hidden in the lines of dialogue.

Actors should dig deep into the text when they are creating a character and never make easy-option decisions based on lazy thinking.

4

Research

IAGO. ... strong circumstances
Which lead directly to the door of truth...

Othello (3.3)

RESEARCH IS AN EXTREMELY USEFUL TOOL FOR ACTORS when they are in the process of creating a performance. It can give them loads of information about the world the characters inhabit, the culture in which the story is set, and the politics of the era. An investigation into the writer's own life will also help the actors understand the characters in the play and why they behave as they do. And visual research can reveal interesting facts about buildings, transportation and the clothes that the characters would wear. In fact, the deeper the research, the more rewarding the results.

But research can be more than just an information provider; it can also be a stimulus to the actor's creative muse. When actors are preparing for a performance in a play or film, they often find that ideas come from unexpected places. It could be an item of news on the television; a stranger they see walking down the street; a phone call from an old friend; a song on the radio. Anything. A random incident which doesn't have any connection to the production may suddenly give the actor an inspirational idea about their character.

And these moments of inspiration can sometimes pop up when an actor is carrying out a piece of research. Even a mundane investigation can sometimes cause a brilliant idea to spring into the actor's mind. It may have nothing to do with any particular area of research, but because the actor's imagination is open to new ideas, creative inspiration is in free-flow. A photograph in a book. An article on Wikipedia. A video on YouTube. And kapow! A sudden brainwave that the actor would never have had without it.

It's important to realise that research is not only useful and informative; it is also an indispensable part of the creative process because it is the yeast in the actor's creative dough.

The Writer

What was the writer trying to say and what influenced their thinking?

If the actors understand what the writer was trying to say, and why he or she was trying to say it, they are more likely to convey this clearly in performance. Research into a writer's life, other work and their artistic influences will give a greater understanding of the work being rehearsed.

Biographies

Studying the life of writers and the people they knew can often give a tremendous insight into the characters and the plots of their plays.

Let's face it: what happens to us in our life has a major impact on our understanding of the world. So it is inevitable that a writer will tap into his or her own experiences in the development of characters and plot. Eugene O'Neill, for instance, dramatised whole periods of his own life in plays such as *The Iceman Cometh*, *Long Day's Journey into Night* and *A Moon for the Misbegotten*. And writers like Harold Pinter and John Osborne often created characters based on the people they knew.

The Writer's Other Work

The understanding of a particular play can be enhanced by examining the themes, characters, relationships and plots of other scripts by the same writer.

Writers often explore similar themes and plots in their work. For instance, Alan Ayckbourn often satirises middle-class aspirations in his plays. Harold Pinter unravels with the way we attempt to communicate with each other – or fail to communicate. Similar characters sometimes crop up in different circumstances, like the faded Southern beauty who appears in several of Tennessee Williams's plays and films. The same relationship may be explored in a variety of ways. With increased knowledge of the writer's other work, it is possible to build a greater understanding of the characters in their plays.

The Writer's Contemporaries

Cultural trends, social conventions and artistic ambitions are often mirrored in the plays of writers from the same period.

Writers who have stood the test of time usually fall into two categories. They were either the masters of the prevailing theatrical style or they bucked the current trend and created a new kind of theatre. Sometimes they were in both categories. They created a new form of theatre, and immediately became the best exponent of the new style. Look at the plays of Oscar Wilde or Noël Coward. When they had their successes, other writers jumped on the bandwagon and wrote comedies of manners with witty dialogue, but none of the other writers did it as well as Wilde or Coward.

Plays written by the writer's contemporaries can also reveal how astonishing and original the writer's work was at the time it was first performed. If you read other Elizabethan plays, you will see how Shakespeare's play *Hamlet* would have shocked the Elizabethan audiences. It was, and still is, an enigmatic exploration of a troubled and indecisive mind, but Elizabethan audiences had never seen a play with such an irresolute main character. The prevailing style was to write about people who knew who they were and said what they wanted. So when Hamlet walked on the stage and said he didn't know exactly how he was feeling and he wasn't sure what he should do next, the Elizabethan audiences must have been amazed. What sort of hero is that?

If you understand the impact that a play had on its first audiences, you can start to find ways to recreate that impact for a modern audience. Hamlet is often seen as a rather melancholy exploration of madness, but for the Elizabethan audience it was a shocker. Something to wake them up and make them start thinking.

Visual Imagery

What did the world look like to the characters in the play?

Photographs and Films

When researching a story that takes place from the late nineteenth century onwards, photographs and documentary films are a tremendous source of information. This visual imagery can be found quite easily on the internet and in libraries. But some archived photographs can be rather deceptive because they depict extremes of chic that only the fashion-conscious rich could afford. So care should be taken to ensure that the photographs are of real people in a real environment. Similarly, documentary films are better for research than fictional films because they are more likely to present an accurate depiction of the world, rather than an idealised or romanticised version created by an art director.

Paintings and Illustrations

Paintings and illustrations can also be quite deceptive. Of course, if an actor is about to play Henry VIII or Elizabeth I, he or she will be able to get some idea of how they dressed and where they lived by looking at contemporary paintings of them in the National Portrait Gallery. Even if an actor is playing a fictional, high-ranking character from the past, there will probably be paintings of posh interiors and people wearing expensive clothing. The trouble is that poor people didn't get their portraits painted.

However, some artists from the past did depict people the way they really were. Some Dutch painters like Frans Hals and Adriaen van Ostade, for instance, would often paint ordinary people in ordinary places. And in Britain, William Hogarth with his extraordinary sequence of illustrations in *The Rake's Progress* and *Industry and Idleness* gave us an insight into the way people actually dressed in the early eighteenth century and what they really looked like.

Newspapers

Photographs and illustrations from newspapers can often be a useful resource for visual research. They also contain written information that may give an insight into a particular era. Some libraries have bound copies of old newspapers and magazines, and many of them are being made available on the internet.

Fashion and Clothing

How would a character dress? How would their clothes affect their physicality? Does their clothing have any bearing on their self-image?

In an ideal situation, the actors will work with a costume designer to find the appropriate clothing for their characters. But on other occasions the actors will simply be provided with costumes or be in the position of having to find their own. But whichever of these situations the actors find themselves in, the more knowledge they have about the clothing of the period, the more they will understand how their own character would dress.

Styles

Styles of clothing from a particular period can have a tremendous impact on the people who are wearing them, but it is important for an actor to make sure they understand the extent of their character's interest in clothing. Look around you. How many people are wearing ultra-fashionable clothes these days? Not many. And they are usually pretty young. The rest of the population wear an assortment of rather ordinary items: jeans, sweaters, suits. Most people spend their lives wearing the same unfashionable clothes they wore when they were in their late teens and early twenties.

It is also worth considering the sort of work that people do. Does an estate agent wear the same sort of clothes as a plumber? Of course not. And two hundred years ago would a clerk have worn the same clothes as a carpenter? No. Class, position and occupation all have an impact on the kind of clothes that people wear.

So looking back in time to a particular period of history, it may be possible to identify the fashionable clothing of the time, but it's important to remember the following:

- Not many people actually wear 'high fashion'.
- Older people tend to wear styles that were popular when they were young.
- The way people dress is often closely related to their occupations.

Materials and Undergarments

Silk feels different from cotton. Velvet has quite a different weight from wool. Brocade is heavy and stiff, whereas satin is light and cold to the touch. It is important to know what materials the clothes of a particular period would have been made from because it will affect the way a character moves. If a dress is made of heavy brocade, it will be quite an effort to lug it about. Movement will have to be slow and precise. On the other hand, if a dress is made of silk, it will be light and flowing, and movement will be unrestricted.

Similarly, undergarments will affect the way a person moves. Stiff, tight corsets are extremely restricting, particularly of the upper body. Sometimes seventeenth- and eighteenth-century corsets were so tight that it was impossible to fill the lungs properly. No wonder women were continually passing out. The big hooped skirts that eighteenth-century women sometimes wore must have been really difficult to manoeuvre. They would hardly have been able to sit down. And even then they would have had to perch on the edge of an upright chair and be careful that the whole thing didn't spring up in the air. Really difficult.

Jewellery, Accessories and Make-up

What sort of jewellery did people wear? What did people carry around with them? How much make-up did they wear? (And was make-up purely for women?) In the late seventeenth and early eighteenth centuries, rich women often carried fans around to waft in front of their faces, and men used handkerchiefs quite flamboyantly to express themselves. And why was this? Well, there was no dry-cleaning in those days and expensive clothing couldn't be washed properly, so after a while it must have smelled pretty bad. The ladies' fans and the gentlemen's handkerchiefs were very expressive accessories that could be used in all manner of ways, but when they were doused in perfume and waved in front of your face, they could also help to ward off all manner of evil odours.

It's also worth finding out what personal objects people would have had with them. Did they carry around fob watches, did they wear wristwatches or would they find out the time by looking at a clock? And how about glasses? If glasses were expensive and not very good, that must have meant that some people would have had a very blurred view of the world and that would have affected the way they looked at other people. It could even affect the way they moved around the room. In the past, people would have written with a quill pen. That means they would have had to sharpen the nib and they would have had to know how to do that. How often did a nib need sharpening? How often was a quill replaced? People would certainly have carried penknives around with them in order to keep their pens in good nick.

Then there were snuff boxes in some periods. Cigarette cases in others. Lighters. Matches. Little notebooks. After Hamlet has seen the ghost of his father, he says, 'My tables: meet it is I set it down…', and then he writes in a little book, his 'tables' (1.5). But what did he write with? And what would the notebook be like?

The design and construction of personal objects tells us a lot about an era, and as props they can give an actor plenty of scope for physical action and a true sense of the period of the play or film.

Hairstyles and Beards

Tightly coiffed hair held in place with pins and oils feels very different from a shaved head or loose romantic curls. Did men grow beards and/or moustaches, and how thick would they have been? What does it feel like to have a waxed moustache? Were wigs popular and why? Apparently some complicated eighteenth-century wigs for women were built on bamboo frames like a guardsman's bearskin. How on earth did they keep them in place and what must it have felt like?

Architecture and Transport

What did the buildings look like, both inside and out? How did people get from one place to another?

Buildings

The buildings people live in affect the way they behave. If you are accustomed to large, airy rooms with high ceilings, you may feel more expansive and important, whereas a cramped hovel will lower your spirits and may even give you a permanent stoop. A person who is used to elegance and grandeur will feel uncomfortable in a worker's cottage and vice versa. A semi-detached suburban home will feel very different from a crowded, rambling farmhouse, and each will have an effect on the people who live in them.

Interior Decor and Furniture

What does the interior of a room look like and what sort of furniture would it have? Are the chairs comfortable? Is the furniture sturdy? In some periods, a room would be oppressively full of ornaments and pictures, while in others it would be generally bright, light and empty. If a character is playing a scene in a cold stone hall with an enormous fireplace blasting out heat, it would be quite a different atmosphere from being in a cosy, snug sitting room.

Domestic Appliances

Domestic appliances have been quite different in different periods of history, so it is important to know what a character would actually be using and how they would use it. For instance, in Noël Coward's play *The Vortex*, the character of Nicky keeps putting different records on the gramophone. But it wouldn't have been as simple in the 1920s as it is now. First of all, he would have selected a brittle, breakable ten-inch shellac disc from the shelf. Then he would have carefully removed its cardboard cover and put the disc on a green-felt turntable. Finally, he would have had to replace the used steel needle with a new one and wind up the clockwork mechanism, before manoeuvring the heavy pick-up arm over the record and placing the needle carefully in the groove. What a palaver! And all that for only three-and-a-half minutes of music.

Personal and Public Transport

How would a character get about and how would that affect their clothing and their physical well-being? If they have travelled by horse before they arrive in a scene, they could be weary, muddy and sore. If they have travelled by taxi, they may be relaxed and smartly dressed. Omnibuses would have been crowded and smelly, and trains would have been interminably slow. If a character has arrived by some sort of transport it will, of course, affect the way they feel as they enter a scene.

Blue-screen and CGI

Blue-screen is when the actors are filmed performing a scene without being on an actual set at all. They are literally filmed in front of a blue screen. The setting is filled in later by digital editors who can replace the blue areas of the picture with any background they like. It's the same with CGI (computer-generated imagery). The actors could be filmed fighting monsters who aren't there at all, in a fantastical world that only exists as a computer-generated image. If actors are filming in these conditions, they would have no idea of their surroundings if they hadn't done the appropriate research, asked the right questions and looked at lots of pictures.

Economics, Politics and Religion

What is the overriding economic and political climate of the time in which a play or film is set? And how much would it have affected the characters?

Caryl Churchill's play *Serious Money* deals with corporate finance and greed in the City of London. Clearly the actors in that play need to research that particular world. *Racing Demon* by David Hare is about the Church of England, and Nick Stafford's adaptation of Michael Morpurgo's novel *War Horse* is about the First World War. Obviously these subjects would need to be fully researched. *The Laramie Project* by Moisés Kaufman and the Tectonic Theater Project, which deals with a homophobic murder, and *The Colour of Justice* by Richard Norton-Taylor, which dramatises the inquiry into the killing of Stephen Lawrence, are based on actual incidents and use transcripts and interviews to create dialogue. The actors in both of these plays would benefit enormously in their quest to present a truthful version of events if they conduct some extensive research.

But some plays are set in the context of a particular political environment without it actually being the main theme. Bertolt Brecht's *Mother Courage and Her Children* is about the effect of war on a group of characters struggling for survival. *Amy's View* by David Hare is set against the evolution of Thatcher's Britain. Even though the political background of these plays is not their primary focus, actors working on either of them would benefit enormously from suitable research.

And although some plays don't have such strong political themes, it's safe to say that most characters in most plays live in a specific time and place where events outside the scope of the play could easily affect the characters' behaviour.

Geography and Climate

The surrounding landscape can have a marked effect on the people who live in the area. It can affect their mood and their outlook on life.

The actors should have a clear vision of the outside world when they are in a play. A busy street outside the door will affect the way a character enters a room quite differently from isolated moorland. The weather may be hot or cold; wet or windy; misty or bright. The climate of an area can affect the way the characters think and behave.

If these things are not outlined in the text of the play, then the actors should get together and make some decisions. These apparently minor details can often bring a play to life.

Society

What rituals, customs and traditions affect a character?

Different societies have markedly different ways of educating their children. They have different cultural rituals concerning birth, marriage and death. Courting rituals vary greatly and there are different attitudes to sex and gender issues. In different societies, people engage in different pastimes and leisure activities when they are not working. Sometimes knowledge of these things is essential in order to get a proper understanding of the way the characters behave in a play. The actors should not assume that their character will have the same attitude to these things that they themselves have.

Art and Science

Who were the major artists at the time, and what were the latest scientific theories and discoveries?

Art is often an expression of the age. Actors can learn a lot about the inner life of their characters by researching works of art created at the time of the play. Contemporary philosophers can also help the actor understand the values and attitudes of the period in which a play is set. Current scientific discoveries could also have an impact on the characters, and it's worth remembering that a character can only know the things that have been discovered or invented up until the time of the play.

There is no telling what area of research will inspire an actor. Sometimes a new bit of knowledge will unexpectedly open up the floodgates of the imagination and the actor will find themselves in the creative zone. Research is not necessarily just a way of collecting interesting facts. When actors are being deeply creative, a new bit of knowledge can sometimes produce 'eureka' moments of discovery.

Research will give the actors a clear understanding of the world of the play, and that in turn will help them reveal the unique and complex inner lives of their characters.

5

Creating a Character

HAMLET. ...God hath given you one face, and you make yourself another...

Hamlet (3.1)

Like explorers embarking on an expedition into unknown territory, all the maps of the surrounding area have been examined and all the appropriate equipment has been gathered together. Experts have been consulted and facts have been analysed. With the research completed, it is now time to take the first steps on the journey. It's time for the actor to get creative. Try things out. Make things up. And be inventive.

When painters are preparing new works, they will often make sketches of their ideas. They'll draw a bit, think about what they've done, set the sketch aside and draw some more. Eventually, as a result of these sketches, a complete picture will form in the painter's mind, and they will start to mix their paints and apply them to the canvas.

The following exercises are like a series of painter's sketches. They stimulate the actor's imagination and give them the opportunity to try things out. Each actor will respond differently, but all the exercises are worth trying because no one knows what will happen without giving them a shot.

Character Questions

Actors have to understand what it is like to be someone other than themselves – and that is very complicated. A character in a play exists for about two-and-a-half hours and that is all we know about them. But real people are moulded by a lifetime of experience, so in order to make a character truly believable, the actor has to think about that person's life outside the confines of the play.

There are a lot of questions about character in the following questionnaire. Some of them are very straightforward and the answers can be gleaned from the text, but others will need an imaginative response. Like a poet, an actor must allow their imagination to flow. They should smile at incongruities. They should try out wild ideas and see if they'll fit. After all, acting is fun, and there is no reason why actors shouldn't delight in imaginative answers to these questions.

The Character Questionnaire

Each actor, in character, writes answers to the following questions, letting their instincts, imagination and creativity come into play.

If this is done as part of the rehearsal process, then the actors should have at least two hours in order to be able to consider all the questions properly. If it is done outside of rehearsals, then the answers can be as long as the actors like.

It can be even more interesting to add 'and why?' to the end of some of the questions, as in 'What is your biggest fear… and why?' Of course, this will take a lot longer.

For the sake of clarity it's advisable to write each question out and then follow it with the answer.

Your History

1. *What is your full name?*
2. *Do you have a nickname?*
3. *If you have a nickname, how did you get it?*
4. *How old are you?*
5. *How does your age affect your feelings about yourself?*
6. *Who are your closest relatives?*
7. *How do they affect or influence you?*
8. *What kind of education did you have?*
9. *How did your education affect or influence you?*
10. *How did you enjoy your childhood?*
11. *What is the worst thing you have ever done?*
12. *What is the best thing you have ever done?*
13. *Have you travelled much?*

Your Present Circumstances

14. *Are you married, single, divorced or separated?*
15. *How do you feel about your marital state?*
16. *Do you live with someone or do you live alone?*
17. *Do you have any children?*
18. *How do you feel about this?*
19. *Where do you live and what is it like?*
20. *How do you feel about where you live?*
22. *Who is your best friend?*
23. *What is your social life like?*
24. *How do you feel about your social life?*
25. *What sort of people are you most comfortable with?*
25. *What sort of people annoy you?*
26. *What sort of work do you do?*
27. *How does your work affect your social status?*

28. *Are you lazy or are you a workaholic?*
29. *What frustrates you?*
30. *What is your greatest responsibility?*
31. *What qualities do you admire in others?*
32. *Are you independent/self-sufficient?*
33. *Are you an honest person?*
34. *What are your most and least attractive qualities?*

The Future

35. *What are your ambitions – short-, medium-, long-term?*
36. *Are you confident about future success?*
37. *Are you confident about future happiness?*
38. *How would a large inheritance or a big win in the lottery affect you?*
39. *What would you do if you became heavily in debt?*
40. *What would you change about your life if you could?*
41. *What would you change about the world if you could?*
42. *How would you like to be remembered after your death?*

Your Physical and Vocal Qualities

43. *What are your physical abilities?*
44. *What is your voice like?*
45. *What physical impression do you give to other people?*
46. *What is your laugh like?*
47. *What is your energy level?*
48. *How does your work affect you physically?*
49. *What is your state of health?*
50. *How sexual/sensual are you?*
51. *Do you take care of your personal appearance?*
52. *What are your most and least attractive features?*

Your Emotional Qualities

53. *How would you describe your temperament?*
54. *How does your work affect your mental health?*
55. *How sensitive are you?*
56. *How confident are you?*
57. *What is your biggest fear?*
58. *What do you worry about?*
59. *Are you vain?*
60. *What makes you envious?*
61. *What makes you embarrassed?*
62. *Are you an introvert or an extrovert?*
63. *Are you an optimist or a pessimist?*
64. *What makes you angry?*
65. *What makes you laugh?*
66. *What makes you cry?*

Your Intellectual Qualities

67. *How would you describe your intellectual process?*
68. *Are you logical or illogical?*
69. *What are your spiritual or religious beliefs?*
70. *Are you outspoken about your beliefs?*
71. *What are you secret about?*
72. *Are you a good liar?*
73. *What do you daydream about?*

Your Likes and Dislikes

74. *What is your favourite food and drink?*
75. *What is your favourite time of day?*
76. *Which is your favourite season?*
77. *What is your favourite topic of conversation?*
78. *What is your least favourite topic of conversation?*

79. *What bores you most?*
80. *What stimulates you most?*
81. *What do you worry about?*
82. *What is your sexual orientation?*
83. *How do you feel about sex?*
84. *Are you most at ease with members of your own sex or members of the opposite sex?*
85. *Do you like adventure?*

Questionnaire Analysis

The day after the questionnaire has been completed, the actor reads through the answers to get an overview of the way their creative ideas have developed.

If possible, each actor should read some of their answers out to the other members of the cast so it can form the stimulus for an open discussion. Other actors may have useful ideas, and, as the group works together, character relationships will start to evolve.

Physical Explorations

Finding a physicality that suits a character is a potent method of becoming someone else. The body is a fantastic tool for exploration and a physical change can make an actor feel quite different. Physicality and personality often walk hand in hand. Each affects the other. Each is dependent on the other.

Observation

The actors should ask themselves if their character is like anyone they know.

A person's physicality is often governed by psychological characteristics. For instance, a defensive nature may give a person hunched-up shoulders and a shuffle in the way they walk. So if a person's physicality is closely connected to their inner life, then it's possible for an actor to get an understanding of that inner life by adopting a particular physicality. Hunched shoulders and a shuffling walk could make an actor begin to understand a defensive personality.

During the course of rehearsals an actor may realise that their character has a similar disposition to a person that they know. Maybe it's a passion for life. Maybe it's an obsession with making money or an interest in sport. If the actor does find someone like their character, they should observe them and see if they can copy that person's physical rhythms, movements and shapes. As they do this, they may start to get a feeling of that person's psychological and emotional view of the world.

Having found the essential physicality of that person, the actor can try exploring different activities. For instance, they can imagine that they are strolling in the sunshine, going shopping or running for a bus. They can explore how this new physicalisation affects the way they sit on a chair or enter a crowded room. If they are working with other actors, they can see what it is like to greet a stranger or meet an old friend, all the time monitoring what their body language is telling them about their character, and analysing their instinctive behaviour to see what they can learn from it.

Animals

The actors should ask themselves what animal their character is most like.

Anyone who has a pet knows that animals seem to possess human characteristics. A dog behaves as if it's man's best friend. Cats are seen as independent creatures who can be rather disdainful of human beings. Parrots behave as if they are talking to you. Actually, they do talk to you. But do they know what they are saying? Of course not. It's all very misleading. Although we know it's not true, we often treat animals as if they are like slightly dumb human beings.

Conversely, we often think that humans have animal characteristics. We say that a person is 'feline', or someone is 'mousey', or 'birdlike'. We describe children as 'naughty monkeys', and we say things like

'His bark is worse than his bite' and 'She's getting ready to pounce.' We associate human beings with animals all the time.

So when an actor is trying to get to grips with the creation of a character, it can be quite helpful to see if they can find an animal that appears to have some of the qualities of their character. Professional actors often use this technique. Antony Sher famously studied a spider when he was working on Richard III (I heartily recommend the journal he wrote about that process – a book called *Year of the King*). Sher used both the physicality of a spider, making his Richard scuttle about on crutches, which gave him an extra pair of legs – and the inner life of a spider as he mentally wove an intricate web to capture his prey. Laurence Olivier, who was suffering from arthritis when he was rehearsing Othello, studied a panther to help him create the lithe physicality of the Moor. Anthony Hopkins used both a tarantula and a crocodile when he created Hannibal Lecter on-screen in *The Silence of the Lambs*. A crocodile keeps totally motionless as it lies in wait for a victim, and then it strikes to kill swiftly and violently. I remember the chilling moment when Jodie Foster goes to visit him in prison for the first time, and he is motionless in his cell waiting for her to arrive. Just watching. Like a crocodile. And that evil sipping sound that Hopkins made was how he imagined a tarantula would sound when it was sucking the blood out of its prey.

When actors first start observing animals, they should try to see if they can understand how their chosen animal views the world. Get inside the head of the animal. See if they can figure out its thinking process. There's a lot to be discovered in the eyes of an animal. The way it looks at you, the way it looks at other animals. The way it tilts its head or moves its neck. The way it fixes its stare on a point in the distance and then flicks its eyes to examine something close by. It's also useful to examine the physical rhythm of the animal. How fast does its heart beat? Are its reactions swift or lethargic? Is it calm or alert? Is it the hunter or the prey?

But most importantly, what is it thinking? What is the 'inner life' of the animal you are studying? Of course, it's impossible to know what an animal really thinks, but by closely examining the minute details of an animal's behaviour, an actor can create their own version of the animal's 'inner life'.

Once an actor has found the physicality and inner life of their chosen animal, they can apply it to their character. The best way to do this is to see if they can transform themselves into their animal as accurately as possible, moving around, sitting still, thinking, observing the world, and so on. Then, when they feel as if they have become their animal, they can slowly allow themselves to transform into a more human shape without losing the essence of the animal. Having done that, this new-found physicality can be applied to their character to see what happens. As before, different physical activities can be tried, such as running, walking, sitting in a chair, etc. All the time, the actor should think about what the animal's body language is telling them about their character. They should analyse their instinctive behaviour and see what they can learn from it.

Mannerisms

What mannerisms or idiosyncratic physical habits does a character have?

In order to get by in life, we have all developed strategies to help us deal with the outside world. Sometimes we want to give a physical expression to an aspect of our personality, so that people will understand who we are. Sometimes we have developed mannerisms to protect ourselves from the scrutiny of other people. Sometimes our mannerisms have developed as a result of external influences.

These mannerisms or physical habits can be explored to help an actor find a physical focus for their character.

Expressive Mannerisms

Expressive mannerisms are habits that people have developed to indicate who they are, or who they want other people to think they are. For instance, someone who wants other people to know that they are really listening may be in the habit of nodding their head up and down when people talk to them. This is a physical expression of their desire to let the other person think that they are an intelligent listener. Another person may smile excessively when they are talking, which may scream out, 'Like me! Like me!'

When someone holds their hands palm up it can express a generosity of spirit, and someone who continually wags a pointed finger as they talk is often trying to make themselves seem positive.

Expressive mannerisms can be entirely involuntary; people don't even know they are doing them. You often see a nervous or hyperactive person tapping their heel rapidly up and down as they are sitting, or drumming their fingers on a surface. Sometimes these very same mannerisms express other inner emotions. Happiness, for instance, or excitement.

As the actor begins to discover the inner life of their character, these mannerisms can help them create a physical expression of the character's underlying personality.

Protective Mannerisms

Playing with a strand of hair and perhaps holding it in front of your face as you do it is an obvious protective mannerism, as is holding your hand in front of your mouth or stroking your lips.

Biting your nails is a very effective way of shielding yourself from others, in that it covers up your face and at the same time gives you something to do. Defensive people often put their fingers in their mouths. It's similar to sucking your thumb, which, of course, refers right back to breastfeeding, when you were protected by your mother.

As I mentioned before, hunched shoulders are an obvious protective habit, but not making direct eye contact is also protective. There are many variations on the way people protect themselves through various physical mannerisms.

Symptomatic Mannerisms

Sometimes people have mannerisms that are the direct result of things that have happened to them in the past. A person who has hurt their knee at some time in their life may continually rub it whenever they are sitting down. Some people blink a lot, maybe because their eyes are tired or they got into the habit because they needed glasses. Some people suck their teeth, maybe as the direct result of previous dental problems. Rolling one's neck around could be the result of a headache or stiffness or a previous neck injury.

Some symptomatic mannerisms are the result of previous emotional experiences. Holding a palm of a hand out to stop another person talking could be the result of feeling that no one will listen. Continually glancing around could be symptomatic of a person who has reason not to trust the outside world.

As an actor builds up a picture of their character, it is possible to express some aspects of the character's personality through a physical mannerism of some sort. This will give the actor a physical point of concentration that will go hand in hand with the character's psychological life.

Centres

Where is a character's quintessential centre?

A person's body mass generally has its central point of physical balance somewhere inside the lower torso behind the belly button. This varies, of course, depending on the physical shape of a person, but in the weightlessness of zero gravity the physical centre is the point around which the whole body rotates – its point of equilibrium.

But the quintessential centre of a person isn't a true point of balance; it is the point around which a person's *essential being* is balanced, and it is created by life's experiences.

The quintessential centre has an effect on the way their body moves through the world. For instance, the confident swagger of *shoulders* which navigate the body through imagined crowds; overexpressive *hands* drawing patterns in the air to communicate unarticulated thoughts; the sexual provocation of a fluid *pelvis*; a body rooted too firmly to the ground by the imagined weight of the *lower legs and feet*; thoughts floating in aesthetic dreams as the quintessential centre orbits the *head*; a centre firmly placed deep within the *brain* to analyse and clarify the complications of the world.

If actors use their imagination to place a quintessential centre somewhere in their bodies other than their own quintessential centre, everything changes. They feel different, their movements are different and their view of the world is different. And they can use this shift of centre to explore their character. Malvolio's centre could be at the tip of his nose; Macbeth's in his murderous hands;

Titania's in her heart. These are reasonably obvious choices, but if an actor were to make a more experimental choice of centre, it may capture a more interesting physical aspect of their character. Maybe an actor playing Malvolio will discover that they feel comfortable with a centre in his knees or his elbows. No one else can tell an actor where their character's centre is; it's something they have to feel for themselves.

As with all these explorations, once an actor has found a centre to work with, they can try the physical explorations like running, strolling or sitting.

Energy States

What is a character's energy state?

We all move to a different rhythm, or 'energy state'. Some people are so speedy they get a million things done by multitasking, while other people are so relaxed they are almost horizontal. The lucky ones have their lives in control and have just the right amount of energy for any given task. Maybe each of us is born with an internal clock beating to a certain rhythm, or maybe we develop a rhythm as we are growing up to help us get through life.

I think it is an interesting idea for an actor to see if they can alter their internal rhythm to suit the character they are trying to create. In order to explore this idea, actors should explore where their character fits within a scale of energy that goes from *catatonic*, where a person has no energy at all and is physically immovable, to *rigid*, where their internal energy is so hyper that their body short-circuits and goes into deadlock. It is important to realise that these energy states refer to habitual internal rhythms that people have, and not their emotional reactions to particular events.

Before applying these to a character it is worth exploring each of these energy states separately:

Catatonic

The actor should imagine, really imagine, that they have no energy at all and then see what happens. First of all they will find themselves standing still. They won't even be able to talk, because that takes energy. Then they will realise that they are expending a certain amount of energy holding their body up, so they will slip to the floor and lie down. As they lie there trying to relax, any tensions in the body will drop away, and they will find that the only energy they are expending is the energy that keeps their heart beating and their lungs working. This is not a very useful state for an actor. Unless they are playing a corpse!

Lethargic

This is the energy that people have when they do as little as possible in order to get by. A person with a lethargic energy state would very rarely find the need to run for a bus. They would sit whenever possible and speak in a low voice using as little lung power as they need to get the words out. When they walk, they would almost drag their feet as they take the shortest route on only absolutely necessary journeys. This would be their natural pace. Their favoured energy state. Slumped. Heart beating slowly. Apparently half-asleep. On the other hand, it would be wrong to think that a lethargic person couldn't get excited about something. Or fall in love. Or hurry to an important meeting. What is interesting in exploring these energy states is to discover the internal tempo that affects both the physicality of a character as well as their mental energy, and then experiment with how this might operate in a crisis. Find out how a lethargic person jumps for joy!

Laid-back

This expression was apparently coined in the 1960s to describe a relaxed, effortless way of being which was part of the social revolution happening in America. It was in direct contrast to the work ethic of the previous decade. 'Turn on, tune in, and drop out,' said the American psychologist Timothy Leary, and that's when the expression 'laid-back' became the mantra of his generation. It's an easy-come, easy-go rhythm. Everything is possible if you relax, breathe deeply and let your mind do the thinking for you. No hassle. The great thing about having a laid-back energy state is that you can work with it and achieve things. It's notoriously popular in Los Angeles, where you can meet someone at a party one day, and the next you are planning to make a film together as you sit by the pool. It all appears to be so easy. Nothing is desperate for a person with a laid-back energy state. They are wide awake and totally relaxed.

Efficient

An efficient person gets things done. It may not be exciting, but it will be carefully considered. Like an energy-efficient car, it will get you where you want to go, but it doesn't turn heads as you drive by. It's just the right amount of energy for the job. No more, no less. It's economic. A person with an efficient energy state will weigh up the options and make a well-balanced decision about the most effective way to proceed. It's pedantic and precise. Intelligent but rather lacking in emotion.

Neutral

Ahh! Neutral. The balance of the yin and the yang. The perfect harmony in all things. This energy state is not bland and unexciting; it is neutral because it contains everything. A person with a neutral energy state can be all things to all men. The archetypal hero. The perfect heroine. Violent and brave one minute, sensitive and caring the next. This person will always want to help you solve your problems, even if that means exposing their own weaknesses as they do so. Neutral is the way we would all like to be. It's the way a lot of us erroneously think we are. It's balanced, harmonious and ideal.

Alert

A person who is alert is totally aware of their surroundings. They are the first to hear the phone ring and the last to get bored. There is always something new to consider. A tiny movement seen on the edge of sight. A new idea on the tip of a tongue. An alert person doesn't just make a journey, they live every moment of the journey and take in all the details. Not only that, but they remember it all. They are wise to every nuance in a conversation and they never miss a trick. They are sharp. Bright. Intelligent. Ready for action and totally in control.

Passionate

This is a person who feasts greedily on the banquet of life. Every course is a delicious excitement that makes them overindulge without thinking about the consequences. Living for the moment because life is to be lived. The Beat poet Jack Kerouac hot-diggedy-dog zigging down endless empty highways in search of… what?

Who cares? He just wants to be free. No responsibilities. Lapping up life and loving every unfamiliar mystery. The passion and excitement of every encounter and any occurrence.

Ecstatic

When the excitement gets out of control a person can be described as having an ecstatic energy state. This is when their experience of life is metaphysical. It has nothing to do with reality and everything to do with the inexplicable, and they want to tell everyone about it. Ecstatic people *believe* in things. They sometimes gesture wildly with their hands because words are not enough. They grasp fistfuls of air as if they are scooping up the meaning of life and presenting it like a piece of raw, bloody flesh. Letting it ooze between their fingers. Making an unholy mess, and revelling in the chaos, their energy barely in control. A ecstatic person indulges in the vast enigma of the universe. Mystical, mystified and full of ecstasy!

Hysterical

When the energy is out of control, a person can be described as hysterical. Nothing makes sense. Thoughts and ideas tumble on top of each other, spilling out like overripe fruit from a jam-packed cornucopia, splattering onto the floor and walls, destroyed and undigested. Each unformed thought is supplanted by the next before it has time to mature and solidify. Millions of ideas but no wisdom. The brain is a cauldron of bubbling nonsense trying desperately to keep the world in focus.

Rigid

Short circuit! No control over anything. The energy is so intense that the body and the mind blow a fuse. Nothing works. Total tension as the energy fights itself, doubles and then trebles its intensity and solidifies the physical and mental processes like a piece of amber. This is a state of inaction. Of rigidity. Of total lack of movement and total inability to move.

Using Energy States

As I said, when using these energy states it is important to realise that they refer to a character's habitual internal rhythms and not their emotional reaction to particular events. A person who could be described as having a neutral energy state can sometimes feel passionate about something and on other occasions they can feel lethargic. Whatever their habitual energy state may be, it's interesting to see how people deal with the emotional ups and downs of life. The thought process of an hysterical person may be a jumble of unformed ideas, or the world view of a laid-back person could be described as relaxed and easy-going, but at some time in their lives they will get angry, or fall in love, or plan a complicated holiday. Or any of a million different life experiences. And it's the way that people handle these different experiences that makes them into complex and interesting human beings.

These energy states can be explored using the rather poetic hints I have given in the descriptions. Then it will be interesting to see how a character with a particular energy state deals with various everyday experiences. How does a lethargic person run for the bus when they are determined not to be late? How does an ecstatic person relax in the sun? What does an alert person do when they are distracted by romantic thoughts? These ideas can be explored through improvisation when an actor is working on a specific character.

Frankenstein's Monster

The story of *Frankenstein* is about a man who wanted to create life. Let's face it, that is what actors do when they are in the process of creating a character. Unfortunately, Dr Frankenstein's experiment went wrong. His idea was to gather up different body parts from dead people and join them all together to make a perfect human being. He had no intention of creating a monster. In fact, in the way the story is told in various film adaptations, he was trying to get the best organs and limbs he could find. The legs of a champion runner, the shoulders of a weightlifter, the heart of a lover. Unfortunately, when he sent his assistant Fritz to get the brain of an intellectual, Fritz dropped it on the way back to the laboratory and it got spoiled. As a replacement, Fritz could only find the brain of a murderer who was hanging on a gallows. He cut it out, took it back and gave it to his master without telling him. Frankenstein sewed it carefully into the skull. And that's how the monster was created.

After exploring the various aspects of character using some or all of the techniques I've described, it is worth spending some time drawing all the discoveries together into the creation of a complete human being. Rather like Dr Frankenstein, but without the incompetent Fritz.

Actors should lie on their backs for this exercise, letting their arms and legs rest comfortably on the floor. They should give themselves a few minutes to empty their minds of any day-to-day concerns and then start thinking about all the character discoveries they have made so far. The physical explorations. The character questions. Anything they have gleaned from the text.

They shouldn't do anything physical. They should just think. Let their minds roam in the creative ether of their imagination.

And as they do that, each actor should allow various aspects of their character to seep into their body. I think it's best to start with the feet so they can feel their character flow up through their body a bit at a time, like a liquid. They should imagine that their feet are becoming the feet of someone else by letting the 'character liquid' flow into them. They should allow their ankles and then their lower legs to have a different feel as the liquid enters their body. There's no hurry. They should keep thinking about the things they have learned so far as they let their character flow up through their knees. Their thighs. Their crutch and their stomach. They should allow their imagination to do the work as they feel their character flow into their chest and shoulders, and down their arms to the very tips of their fingers. They should take time to feel the liquid flow into their major organs. Their heart, lungs and liver. Allowing their heart to beat to a different rhythm and their lungs to expand and contract in a different way. This is all about the power of mind over matter. Imagination. And finally their character liquid flows into their skull, and seeps into their brain and face and their senses. Sight, hearing, taste, touch and smell all respond differently to the surrounding environment.

Then they can open their eyes and see the world the way their character would see it. Listen to the sounds in the room and hear them the way their character would hear them. Think the way their character would think.

They can start to move their body, a bit at a time. First, their fingers and hands. Feeling how different they are. Examining them. Moving them around. Seeing how they flex and grip. How they make a fist and how they drum on the floor. They can try wiggling their toes. Rotating their ankles. Gradually coming alive and examining their new body. Seeing how it works. Sitting up. Rolling their neck. Examining the details of the room the way their character would see them. Standing up the way their character would stand. Letting themselves be someone else. It no longer matters about all the exercises and discoveries they have made so far; this creative moment is all that matters. They shouldn't force preconceived ideas into the exercise any more; they should just behave as their character wants to behave. Observe the world and react to it the way their character would.

Creativity is what is happening in the moment, not something that is planned or devised.

At this point, an actor can keep exploring in any way they want. They can do simple explorations in the room, like running or walking or sitting in a chair. They can talk to people if they are working with other actors. Or they can go outside and experience the world as their character would experience it. Walking in the park. Talking to strangers. Reading a newspaper. Lying in the sun. Anything they like, as long as they continue to imagine that it is their character that is doing all these things.

Written Explorations

So far the written explorations of character have been about answering questions that probably only need single-sentence answers, but longer written explorations will get further inside the head of a character. In a way they are like solo improvisations, because when an actor writes something down it is as if they are trying to communicate their thoughts to someone else.

Their best friend, a bunch of strangers, or even their own future self.

The Character Profile

Each actor should find a song or a piece of music that suits their character and play it in the background while they write the following profiles in character, as if they were part of a diary.

- A brief history of my (i.e. my character's) life.
- How I spend the average day.
- What has happened to me before the play starts
- What I imagine might happen to me after the play ends.
- What I am doing during the parts of the play when I am not onstage.
- My main fears, obsessions and desires.
- My attitude to love/sex/relationships.
- What I feel about the other people in the play.
- My state of health.
- My most and least attractive qualities.
- What I feel about my appearance.

Motivations and Objectives

As the actor discovers more and more about their character, they should also start to think seriously about what motivates their character. (This is the essence of Stanislavsky: the exploration of *objectives*, *obstacles* and *actions*.)

Each actor writes at least a paragraph in answer to the following questions:

- What does my character want:
  - Out of life?
  - Now?
  - To happen next?
  - To become?

– **To change?**

– **To achieve?**

These are the character's *objectives*. They are the driving forces in a character's life.

- **What is the reason my character wants each of these things?**

  This is the *justification for action* for a character. The reasons or motivations behind the wants.

- **What degree of urgency does my character feel about achieving their objectives?**

  This is the *immediacy of action* for a character. Richard III wants everything to happen *now*. It's the first word he says in the play. Hamlet, on the other hand, is continually stalled by inaction: 'Yet I, / A dull and muddy-mettled rascal, peak / Like John-a-dreams, unpregnant of my cause, / and can say nothing' (2.2).

- **What will happen if my character doesn't achieve their objectives soon?**

  This is the *consequences of inaction* for a character. The stakes should be high in order to create drama.

- **What does my character need to overcome?**

  These are the *obstacles to action* for a character. The things that get in the way, whether they are external obstacles like a powerful opponent or the lack of money, or personal obstacles, like a character's own fears, uncertainties or lack of physical strength.

- **What must my character do to get what they want?**

  This is the *action* a character takes to get what they want. Although the script often outlines the major actions that a character takes to achieve their desires, the actor will realise their character's needs by the way they vocalise each line of dialogue and by the physical activities that their character undertakes.

All these different exercises and reflections to create well-rounded characters can either be used in rehearsals or they can be things that the individual actor does as part of their own personal exploration. Some directors will feel that it is the actor's responsibility to work these things out on their own, while others will want to incorporate them into the rehearsal process. Sometimes they may be a prelude to rehearsing the actual scenes, and at other times they may be used in tandem with more conventional rehearsal techniques. But however they are used, the actors will find them extremely productive.

These initial explorations into the creation of a character will provide solid foundations for confident performances.

6

Group Discussions

WILLOUGHBY. Nay, let us share out thoughts as thou
dost ours.

ROSS. Be confident to speak, Northumberland;
We three are but thyself: and, speaking so,
Thy words are but as thoughts; therefore be bold.

Richard II (2.1)

I'VE ALREADY SUGGESTED SEVERAL OCCASIONS WHEN THE actors should get together to discuss various aspects of the play. Any research that an individual actor has done should be shared with the rest of the group, so that everyone is up to speed with the social and political background or the era.

The following suggestions for group discussions will sometimes be a continuation of these conversations, but now the actors can make their own choices about their character. Several of the questions in this chapter deal with beliefs and moral opinions, and some of the actor's choices for their character could be in direct opposition to the prevailing attitudes of the time. A group discussion will give the actor an opportunity to justify their character's attitudes by arguing them through with the rest of the group. It would be easy to say 'My character doesn't believe in the death penalty,' but if the actor has to argue the case for that particular conviction, then they will be forced to consider the implications and consequences of holding such a belief.

Economics

- **How do the characters make a living?**

  This isn't such an obvious question as you might think. Yes, if you're working on a production of *Hobson's Choice*, you can be pretty sure that most of the characters earn a living by making and selling shoes. On the other hand, most of the characters in *The Importance of Being Earnest* don't have to earn a living at all, they are just rich. Some of the smaller characters in the play have to work: Merriman is a butler, Reverend Chasuble is obviously a rector, and Miss Prism is a governess, but what do they actually do? Merriman serves the tea, but did he prepare it? Does Miss Prism teach? And if she does, what is her best subject?

  But these are specific circumstances. We all know that money makes the world go round and it is impossible to live without it, so what the actors need to do is discuss how each of the characters gets their money. How much do they have, how much do they need, and if they work, what do they do to get it and how much time does it take up?

- **What are the characters' attitudes to money?**

  For some people, money is vitally important and for others it's a necessary evil that they try to avoid thinking about. Some people splash money about even if they don't have much, while others are remarkably tight-fisted even if they have a stash. Money creates security, but some people never feel secure unless they are getting more and more. We have loads of phrases to describe how particular people feel about money: spendthrift, miser, tightwad, philanthropist, big spender, etc. It's an emotive subject which often dictates a person's behaviour, so each actor should make a decision about their character's attitude to money.

- **How do the characters spend their money?**

  Do they spend their money on clothes? Or fast cars? Gambling? Holidays? Maybe the characters only earn enough to keep themselves warm, dry and fed. Or maybe they don't even have enough money for that. What would Vladimir and Estragon – the two tramps in Samuel Beckett's *Waiting for Godot* – spend money on if they found some? New shoes? A slap-up meal? A bottle of wine? But being a tramp is an extreme case. Most people have enough money to get by, plus some extra to spend on a few luxuries. The way that the characters in a play or film handle money is another insight into their personalities.

Social Politics

- **What is the power structure amongst the characters in the play?**

Relationships between the characters in a play or film are often influenced by the status that each person may hold in the social order. If we look at an extended family living in a big house with servants, such as you might find in a period drama, the father of the family would tend to be the patriarchal figure and would perhaps have the highest status in the house. But it could be that his ageing dominant mother is living with them, as in the television series *Downton Abbey*. In this case there is a conflict of power, since the male of the family would traditionally have the higher status. Then, of course, there are the children of the family who, on the one hand, may be able to boss the servants around, while on the other, may have to obey rules that the servants have been told to enforce. The servants will also have their own power struggles amongst each other. As will the children. The permutations are endless.

Then, of course, a character would behave quite differently with a person who is lower than them in the social order than they would with someone who is higher than them. This is often highlighted in films or plays about the army, when a sergeant-major is seen bullying the privates and then behaving in a massively servile manner with the commissioned officers. In 1959, Rod Steiger played the title role in a film called *Al Capone* about the famous Chicago gangster. Having previously played second fiddle to Marlon

Brando in *On the Waterfront*, Steiger grabbed the opportunity of playing the lead role and gave the performance of his life. The film tells the story of the gangster's rise to power from a young, poverty-stricken kid to one of the most feared Mafia leaders of all time. At the beginning of the film, when Capone is a teenager trying to join Johnny Torrio's gang, Steiger is running around, cap-in-hand, opening doors for people, keeping his head lowered and ready to do anything for anyone. Towards the end of the film when Capone is at the height of his success, Steiger is overwhelmingly powerful. Shouting and screaming. Throwing women around. Steiger, who was trained in 'The Method' at the Actors Studio along with Marlon Brando, had a great understanding of the effect that this change of status would have on the character he was playing.

- **What are the gender politics of the time?**

When you are rehearsing a play that is from another cultural era, it is important that all the actors agree about the prevailing gender politics, even if their characters don't subscribe to them.

This is really important because gender politics are a moveable feast. Ask any actress who has played Kate in *The Taming of the Shrew*. It's a great part, full of power, wit and life, and anyone would leap at the chance to play her. The trouble is, she gets 'tamed' at the end of the play by Petruchio and has to deliver a speech (in 5.2) about how she thinks women should behave. She tells everyone: 'Thy husband is thy lord, thy life, thy keeper, / Thy head, thy sovereign…', and then she goes on: 'Such duty as the subject owes the prince, / Even such a woman oweth her husband.' She ends the whole speech by saying: 'And place your hands below your husband's foot; / In token of which duty, if he please, / My hand is ready, may it do him ease.' Well! There are very few people in the West today who would believe that a woman should be servile to her husband, let alone place her hand beneath his foot, and actresses often struggle with how to play this speech. Some have made it ironic, some have made her seem to take on an even higher status than Petruchio as she speaks, and some have cast aside the gender politics of today and gone for a version that would have pleased Elizabethan audiences.

- **What is the power structure in love relationships?**

As we all know, there are many different versions of the way that people in love behave with each other. Each situation is different. Relationships can often survive on a continual unspoken negotiation of power. Sometimes one person is the dominant figure, sometimes the other.

Then there is the way that people in a relationship learn how to get what they want. An apparent supplication can, in fact, be a way of exercising power over another person. Giving status can often be more successful than taking status. Relationships also exist where one person decides to exercise total egocentric power over their partner. Power is a strong magnet and it can make the other person feel safe, but desperate for attention. 'Treat 'em mean, keep 'em keen' is the mantra.

But, generally speaking, good relationships are based on a continually updated power structure which is satisfactory for both partners, while bad ones are based on an unbalanced bias towards one partner's demands at the expense of the other. There are many variations to both positive and negative relationships.

Rituals

- **How do the characters take meals?**

Of all the ritual activities, eating is probably the most public. It's also a ritual that varies from period to period and culture to culture. So the actors need to reach a mutual understanding of how the characters in a play or film would take a meal. Do they cook their own food, or do they have servants who will cook for them? Would they sit around a table in a room designated for eating, or would they have a tray on their laps as they watch television from the sofa? Do they say grace? Do they eat together? Do they often have guests? There are many variations of the eating ritual, and the actors need to discover the socially accepted version appropriate to the play or film. Then they can each decide whether their character conforms to it or not.

- **How do the characters wear their clothes?**

  The actors will already have done a lot of research into the fashions of the period, and some decisions will have been made about the clothes their characters would actually wear. Now it is worth discussing how much each of the characters cares about the way they dress. Some people think carefully about colour coordination, while others just bung on any old thing. Some people's clothes are always new and in good condition, while other people love to wear comfortable things that they've had for years. A character's interest in clothing may be entirely different from the actor's own personal interest.

- **How do the characters deal with children?**

  The way we relate to children can sometimes be quite revealing. Some people just ignore them, while others make them part of any social occasion. Sometimes children are expected to behave like mini-adults, and sometimes they are cosseted and never allowed to grow up. Some are treated like servants, while others are treated like friends. The way that people deal with their offspring is often dictated by the cultural environment. But not always. Sometimes it's simply a matter of personal preference.

  And then there is the way that each character relates to children on a one-to-one basis. Even if there are no children in the script, this is worth exploring. Children are able to see through deceptive behaviour very quickly, so the way a character behaves with children can be an insight into how they behave when they are being honest and direct.

- **How do the characters feel about the older generation?**

  In Western culture there is such a cult of youth that getting old is considered to be some sort of failure, and people go to great lengths to try to turn back the hands of time. But in other cultures, old age is respected and old people are venerated for their wisdom and experience. As above, the actors need to agree on the prevailing attitudes to age in the period and culture of the play or film, but each actor also needs to have some idea of how their particular character feels about old age.

- **How do the characters socialise?**

  As I touched on earlier, eating is often a time for socialising, but so is drinking alcohol, watching football or playing a sport. People sometimes book group outings to the theatre or do courses in pottery or painting simply so they can meet other people.

  The way that people socialise can sometimes be useful when deciding how to set a scene, particularly when you are filming. Maybe a game of squash underpins the dialogue of a scene or maybe it takes place in a crowded restaurant. These settings are obviously not so easy to incorporate when actors are working on a stage play, but a game of cards is possible. Or a game of chess. Sometimes a social event is part of the way a scene is written, like the party scene in *Romeo and Juliet*, but how would the people actually behave in a social event like this? Would there be loads of laughter and flirting, or would the whole thing be rather formal and polite? The way people socialise in the particular culture or period of history is something that actors can use to bring life to a scene.

- **How do the characters participate in religion – if at all?**

  In Shakespeare's *Measure for Measure*, Isabella, who is a novice nun, has a moral dilemma brought about by her religious conviction. Her brother, Claudio, is due to be hanged, but Angelo, the Duke's deputy, says he will spare her brother's life if she will have sex with him. When she tells

Claudio that she isn't going to have sex with Angelo, and that Claudio must therefore die, he is clearly upset. As a novice nun, Isabella's attitude to religion is reasonably straightforward, but how about Angelo and Claudio? The actors need to know how their characters feel about religion before they can properly measure the depth of their own dilemmas.

Arthur Miller's play *The Crucible* is driven by religious belief and it is essential for the cast to have a very clear idea of the prevailing attitudes to religion in the community at the time. It's so specific that if the actors don't have a shared understanding, the play simply won't make sense.

Even if religion is not the main theme of a play or film, it is always worth considering how much it may or may not affect the characters.

Morals

- **What do the characters consider to be right or wrong?**

Different societies have their own customs, traditions and belief systems, and from these come particular moral codes which give people a formula on how to live their lives. Sometimes these can be quite shocking to people from other cultures. For instance, Muslim women are often totally shrouded in their burqas, whereas no one turns a hair about total nudity on some French beaches.

Actors need to have a clear understanding of the social conventions in the world of a play or film, but that doesn't mean that each character will adhere to these conventions or even believe in them. Characters who have to stand up against the crowd and fight for their beliefs are often featured in plays and films. In *An Enemy of the People* by Henrik Ibsen, Dr Stockmann is denounced as a lunatic because he wants to close the financially rewarding spa baths because the water has been contaminated. Everyone turns against him, even his friends and allies. He famously says, 'The strongest man in the world is the man who stands most alone.' Terry Malloy in *On the Waterfront* confronts the all-powerful union bosses against all odds. In the film *Jaws*, Sheriff Brody fights the whole community when he wants to close the tourist beaches of Amity Island after a shark attack.

It's important to consider what would be thought of as morally right or morally wrong in the context of a play or film, and then to discuss what each of the individual characters would have felt about the prevailing moral codes. I suppose the point is: you don't have to agree with the social and political beliefs, but you do have to understand them.

- **What do the characters consider to be legal or illegal?**

Crimes against other people, like murder and robbery, are illegal throughout the world, although the punishment varies. But it's the laws of the land which try to impose moral values on the population that can be most diverse. The laws about alcohol and drugs, for instance. The laws about sex and gender. The marriage laws. The laws about slavery. In some countries it's a capital offence to be caught drink-driving. You can be executed for it! In other countries bigamy is encouraged, while in Britain, of course, it's forbidden. Each country makes its own set of moral laws. These are things that different cultures have very different ideas about and the actors should understand them and know whether their characters are for them or against them.

The film *Milk* is about the gay-rights campaigner Harvey Milk. Obviously the actors in that film had to have a very clear idea about the laws on homosexuality in America in the 1970s. They needed to know to what extent each of the characters might feel threatened. Homosexuality was made legal in Sweden in 1944, whereas in Ireland it wasn't officially decriminalised until 1993, nearly fifty years later. The laws about gay marriage in America vary from state to state. It's these laws, the ones that try to impose a 'moral' point of view on the population, that each actor needs to consider from their character's perspective.

Deep Character

- **What would the characters give their lives for?**

  I asked a group of actors what they themselves would give their lives for. The only American in the group said, 'My country.' None of the English actors said this. They said that they would give their lives for their children, or strong religious or moral beliefs. A lot of them said they wouldn't give their lives for anything, and yet in some cultures people become suicide bombers for their beliefs.

  But the real purpose of this question is for the actor to examine what their character would feel so strongly about that they would be prepared to sacrifice their very existence. This in itself will expose some deeply felt convictions, and it may reveal the inner passion of a character.

- **How do the characters choose to act under pressure?**

  In his book *Story*, Robert McKee says, 'The greatest desires have the greatest risks,' and it's those risks that reveal the depth of a character. Pressure can vary immensely. In *High Noon*, Gary Cooper plays a lawman who is just about to get married. When he hears that someone is coming to kill him, he asks the townsfolk for help but they turn their back on him. He has to face the killer alone on Main Street, fearing that he may make a widow of his bride before they are even married. Pressure. Othello has an epileptic fit in Act Four, Scene One of Shakespeare's play, and eventually kills his wife Desdemona due to the pressure that Iago puts him under. In *The Taming of the Shrew*, Kate resists Petruchio's constant pressure that she be a compliant wife for the whole of play, until she finally succumbs at the end of Act Five.

  Of course, most of the characters in a play or film don't have to respond to this sort of pressure, but if they did, how would they react? Would they fall apart or would they rise to the occasion? Would the pressure reveal something about them that they had never considered before? Would it change them for ever?

Group discussions bring the actors together so they can create a cohesive version of the play or film. Of course, a lot of information will be embedded in the words that the characters actually speak to each other, but a shared understanding of the political environment and the social morality that forms a background to any play or film will result in subtle reactions and physical attitudes which will ultimately be more revealing. The audience will respond to subliminal messages without realising it, but these messages can only exist when the actor has a thorough understanding of their character.

Group discussions underpin the plot, giving all the actors a very clear, shared vision of the world their characters inhabit.

7 Exploring the Text

HORATIO. These are wild and whirling words, my lord...

Hamlet (1.5)

I'VE ALREADY TALKED ABOUT HOW TO MAKE AN INITIAL examination of the text, but now I want to describe how to get beneath the surface of the text with particular reference to the character that an actor might be playing.

First of all, it's important to get a clear understanding of how the script is structured, in order to see where each scene fits into the overall arc of the story. When actors are working on little sections of a script they often find that they lose sight of the bigger picture, so it's important for them to remember how the story unfolds from scene to scene.

And then each individual scene needs to be broken down into small sections to see where the changes of rhythm, mood or tempo lie within the scene. These changes are the pulse of drama and bring everything to life.

Finally, each sentence, phrase, or even single word that a character says needs to be analysed. Everything that writers put into their scripts is carefully considered. Even if a text is poorly crafted there will be clues to character, relationships and action within the words that the writer gives the characters to say. It's the actor's job to bring these words to life and make the audience believe that they are the words that the character wants to use. It may sound obvious, but it's not always the case. Sometimes actors want to change the words: 'My character wouldn't say that.' To which my answer would be: 'If you don't think your character would say that, then you've got your character wrong.' Actors should always use the specific words that the writer has chosen, otherwise there is a danger of ending up with a version of the character that is different from the one that the writer had in mind.

Ideally, this sort of deep exploration should be done with the other actors in the scene, but if that is not possible, then each actor can study the text on their own.

The Rhythmical Shape of the Play

Before studying a particular scene, the actors should read through the play again, referring to their 'first impressions', and reminding themselves of the overall shape of the play. As the story unfolds, they should make notes about the changes of rhythm, mood or tempo – where they occur and how significant they are.

Some actors may find it useful to create a chart of how the rhythm changes with a kind of visual score, like a musician's score for a piece of music. For instance, they could draw a timeline of the whole play on a large piece of paper and then add symbols to indicate a particular rhythm for each scene or section of a scene. Lightning bolts could indicate action and drama, wavy lines could indicate peaceful fluidity, sunshine could indicate happiness, and squiggly swirls could indicate confusion. Sometimes the action of the play will suggest the symbol. For instance, a picture of a coffin, followed by drawings of tear drops, followed by lightning bolts would indicate the changing rhythms from section to section in Ophelia's burial scene in *Hamlet*. Rhythms are very infectious, and it is easy to get caught up in the rhythm of a previous section, but changing the internal rhythms of a play will make the story more dynamic and keep the audience on their toes. If every scene is fast and furious it can be just as tedious as every scene being tranquil and serene.

It's exciting to change rhythms as a story unfolds, and the ability to make those changes can be a powerful tool in the hands of the actors.

Super-objectives

The super-objective is the character's prime motivator. The thing that he or she most wants to achieve. You could say that things like money, power, love, glory or fame, etc., are super-objectives. Hamlet's super-objective could be to get revenge for the death of his father. Romeo's could be to find the perfect partner and get married. Maybe an actor could decide that Sir Toby Belch is trying to have as much fun as possible, so that would become his super-objective. Richard III simply wants to be king.

Actually, let's look at Richard III's super-objective for a moment. Yes, he wants to be king, and he is prepared to do anything – and kill anybody – in order to achieve that objective. But on closer consideration, an actor may come to the conclusion that the thing Richard most wants is to get respect. After all, in his first speech he says that even dogs bark at him as he passes by. The only time he has had any respect previously was on the battlefield, and now that it is peacetime he feels very unsatisfied. It's hard to play the super-objective: 'I want to be king,' but if the actor comes to the conclusion that Richard's super-objective is 'I want to get respect,' it will be an achievable objective and that could be more useful.

When an actor has decided on their character's super-objective, they can bring that feeling on with them whenever they appear in a scene. They may become distracted by the immediate turn of events within a scene, but the super-objective will be at the heart of all their actions.

Units and Objectives

In order to make a detailed examination of a character's immediate objectives the script should be divided up into small sections. For each section, the actor should decide what their character wants; discover what gets in the way of achieving that 'want'; and finally decide what their character does to overcome the problem.

This is part of Stanislavsky's system for analysing the text of a play. Unfortunately, the subject of units and objectives can be rather confusing because there are several different interpretations and translations of Stanislavsky's writing. But the principles remain the same, and the analysis is always revealing.

What follows is an outline of the version that I have found to be the most useful.

Units

The text should be divided up into small sections.

A unit is a part of the text that has a simple completeness. It could be a page of dialogue, a single line, or even a piece of physical action – although it is usually several lines of dialogue. Units are often dictated by changes in the characters' objectives, so it is difficult to identify a unit without considering the objectives. Each is dependent on the other. But because actors can often get a *feel* for the changes in a scene before they have a clear understanding of what actually happens to their character moment by moment, I find it more useful to identify where a unit begins and ends before there is an in-depth analysis of the objectives within that unit.

For practical purposes, the analysis of both units and objectives should be undertaken at the same time.

Any changes of mood or tempo within a scene should be discussed by all the actors whose characters are in the scene, and when a specific change is agreed they should make a note of where that change occurs. That is where one unit ends and another one begins. Although this is often when one character achieves his or her objective, it would be wrong to think that each character will achieve their objective at the same time. One character's objective may continue into the next unit, and maybe the following one as well, as he or she strives unsuccessfully to get what they want. When they do achieve their objective, of course, that will probably be the point when a new unit begins.

Objectives

The actors should write down their characters' objectives for each unit.

Romeo may have a super-objective to find love and settle down, but when he is face to face with Juliet for the first time, his objective is probably to kiss her. When he is in her garden later that night and he is waiting under her balcony at the beginning of the scene (2.1), you could say that his objective is to see her face again. He says:

> 'But soft, what light through yonder window breaks?
> It is the east, and Juliet is the sun.
> Arise, fair sun, and kill the envious moon,
> Who is already sick and pale with grief
> That thou her maid art far more fair than she.
> Be not her maid, since she is envious;
> Her vestal livery is but sick and green,
> And none but fools do wear it; cast it off.'

During the first two lines, Romeo has seen a light at the window and he compares it with the light of dawn just before sunrise. Then for the following six lines he is desperate for Juliet to appear, just like he might be desperate for the sun to rise above the horizon.

Then she appears and he says:

> 'It is my lady, O, it is my love!
> O that she knew she were!'

He's seen her and his objective has changed. Perhaps it could now be simply to express his joy. But almost at once it changes again, when he says:

> 'She speaks, yet she says nothing; what of that?
> Her eye discourses, I will answer it.
> I am too bold, 'tis not to me she speaks.'

The actor could now decide that his objective is to talk to her. And so on and so on. Each of these sections is a unit, and each unit will have its own objective.

I have used expressions like 'perhaps it could be…' or 'the actor could now decide…' because the selection of units and each character's objectives are not set in stone. They are to be discussed and discovered. And the final decisions will be uniquely the actor's own.

Obstacles

Each actor should discover the obstacle that prevents their character from achieving their objective in each unit. There are three kinds of obstacle that characters may have to overcome.

1. The obstacle may be outlined in the given circumstances within the script.

In the scene above from *Romeo and Juliet*, Juliet has still not seen Romeo when she says:

> '…Romeo, doff thy name,
> And for thy name, which is no part of thee,
> Take all myself.'

At which point Romeo's objective could be to take Juliet in his arms and kiss her. He says:

> 'I take thee at thy word.
> Call me but love, and I'll be new baptiz'd;
> Henceforth I never will be Romeo.'

Although his objective may be to take her in his arms, the obstacle could be the fact that she is on her balcony and he is in the garden – he literally can't reach her.

2. The obstacle may be created by another character in the scene.

Later on in the scene, Romeo's objective could be to swear his undying love for Juliet when he says:

> 'Lady, by yonder blessed moon I vow,
> That tips with silver all these fruit-tree tops – '

But she immediately interrupts him and says:

> 'O, swear not by the moon, th'inconstant moon,
> That monthly changes in her circled orb,
> Lest that thy love prove likewise variable.'

So now Juliet has created the obstacle to Romeo achieving his objective, because she won't let him swear his undying love.

3. The character's obstacle may stem from something within them.

Maybe their emotional state is the obstacle, or their own belief system. For instance, later in the same scene, Juliet would like nothing better than an immediate exchange of lovers' vows, but her cautious nature holds her back when she says:

> '... Although I joy in thee,
> I have no joy of this contract tonight,
> It is too rash, too unadvis'd, too sudden,
> Too like the lightning, which doth cease to be
> Ere one can say it lightens.'

So now Juliet's obstacle to her objective is her own cautious nature.

These inner obstacles are often the stuff of drama. The frightened hero. The overenthusiastic lover. The doubtful lawyer.

Actions

Each actor should decide what action their character takes to overcome that blocked objective.

It's these actions that bring the story to life. Sometimes they are obvious and built in to the script, but often they simply inform the way that the actor uses the dialogue. For instance, using the three examples above:

1. The obstacle to Romeo's objective of taking Juliet in his arms is their physical distance, so the actor should decide what action Romeo should take to try to overcome it. He could try climbing the ivy under her window as he speaks. Or he could say the dialogue in such a way as to express his love more forcefully, in an attempt to replace the desired physical contact with a strengthened emotional contact.

2. If the obstacle to Romeo's objective of swearing his undying love is Juliet stopping him, then his action could be to physically express his frustration, or to struggle even to speak the words of the dialogue.

3. If the obstacle to Juliet's objective of exchanging lovers' vows is her own cautious nature, then her action could be to fight her inner turmoil and strengthen her resolve, or maybe it could be to express her deep love for Romeo by the way she uses the dialogue as she says goodnight.

Inner Monologue

Each actor should create a 'thought-script' of their character's reaction to everything that other people say and do. These are the thoughts that lie behind the character's choice of words and actions. Actors should know what their character is thinking at every moment, particularly when their character doesn't have much to say.

There are two important things that an actor needs to remember when they are performing a scene. One is to communicate what their character wants to convey to the other characters, as I have described above, and the other is to listen and respond to the things the other characters say and do. Actors should analyse their character's reaction to everything that is going on around them, moment by moment. In future rehearsals, this may change in response to the way the other actors are behaving, but an early analysis will give a clear understanding of a character's inner thoughts, and that will be a strong foundation to underpin truthful reactions to new or unexpected elements introduced later in rehearsals.

Emotional Memory

Each actor should identify experiences in their own life which are similar to those that their character has to deal with during the course of the play or film.

These may be half-remembered experiences, like the first day at school, or a walk in the countryside, but if they are still in the memory it's probably because they produced a strong emotional reaction at the time. The emotions that we experience when we are growing up are like daubs of colour on our emotional palette. Each new emotion broadens the colour spectrum of an emotional memory. Actors can dip a creative brush into a variety of emotional experiences, sometimes blending them together, and then applying them to the emotional life of their character.

So actors should examine the text moment by moment, taking note of any useful memories. Later on in rehearsals, they can focus on the incident that produced a particular emotion and use it when they rehearse that section of the script.

Improvisation can also be used to explore an emotional experience that the actor may not have had in their own life, and then that improvised emotional memory can be used in the development of a scene. There is more about this in Chapter 10 on improvisation.

> I should point out that this is purely a rehearsal exploration. There are some drama theorists who believe that an actor can be thinking about their own emotional experiences while they are actually performing a scene in front of an audience or a camera, but that is not what I believe. I think that actors can use their emotional memories as part of the creative process, but not in performance. For instance, an actor playing Romeo may have used the emotion memory of the death of a grandparent during an exploratory rehearsal of the scene when Mercutio dies, but in later rehearsals all thoughts of the grandparent must be put to one side. In performance, the actor must get inside the head of their character and think only about the death of the other character. The emotional memory is purely a rehearsal aid.

Actioning the Text

Each line of dialogue is given an action word in order to identify the effect that a character wants to have on the people he or she is talking to.

Although I have previously talked about actions in terms of overcoming obstacles, 'Actioning the Text' is a different technique and should be seen as such. I have used the word 'action' in both instances because these techniques are in common usage, and I don't want to create more confusion by inventing new words. Some actors or directors prefer to use units and objectives, and some prefer to action the text. Like all the techniques in this book, each actor should discover for themselves the ones they find to be the most useful.

What people say and what they actually mean don't always correspond. Take an apparently straightforward question like 'Would you like a cup of coffee?' On first glance you could imagine that the speaker simply wants to know if the other person would like some coffee, but there could be a whole host of deeper impulses beneath the surface of this apparently simple question. The speaker could be trying to beguile the other person, or to welcome them. They could be trying to belittle them, or seduce them, or charm them. This is commonly called the subtext and is a device much used by dramatists to enrich the surface banality of the dialogue.

Subtext is made up of the desires, thoughts and/or emotions that a character feels as they speak, even if they are not expressed in the words they say.

Harold Pinter is the master of this kind of subtext. If you read the opening lines of Scene Three in his play *Betrayal*, the characters appear to be having quite a trivial conversation, but the simple dialogue masks a whole host of emotions. Jerry and Emma are sitting in a flat where they conducted an extra-marital affair which is now more or less over. So when she asks if he can remember when they were last in the flat, she could be challenging him to remember. Or even attacking his bad memory. His reply, 'In the summer, was it?', could be trying to humour her. And when she eventually tells him that it was the beginning of September, there is no doubt that the line contains an underlying criticism of his emotional commitment. 'It was actually extremely cold,' she says. 'It's pretty cold now,' he replies. And he is obviously not referring to the weather.

Each line of dialogue can be played in several different ways, and these differences are governed by the actions that the actor applies; they can usually be summed up by an action word like 'challenge', 'attack', 'humour' or 'criticise'.

An action word is always a transitive verb. In other words, it is a word that can be place between the words 'I' and 'you', as in 'I charm you', 'I encourage you', etc.

Each phrase or sentence of dialogue can be given an action. And this will give the actor a sense of purpose when they are playing a scene. After all, no one says anything to anyone else unless they want to affect the other person in some way.

Here is a list of some actioning words:

Actioning Words

A ABANDON, ABSOLVE, ACCEPT, ACCUSE, ADMIRE, AFFIRM, AGGRAVATE, AGITATE, ALARM, ALERT, ALIENATE, AMUSE, APPALL, APPEASE, APPRAISE, AROUSE, ASSAULT, ATTACK, AVOID, AWAKEN

B BAFFLE, BEFRIEND, BEG, BEGUILE, BELITTLE, BEWITCH, BIND, BLACKMAIL, BLAME, BLESS, BLIND, BLOCK, BOLSTER, BRACE, BRIBE, BRUISE, BULLY, BURDEN

C CAJOLE, CALM, CAPTIVATE, CARESS, CAUTION, CHALLENGE, CHARM, CHASTISE, CHECK, CHEER, CHIDE, CHILL, COAX, COMMAND, COMPELL, COMPLIMENT, CONFRONT, CONFUSE, CONSOLE, CONTACT, CONTEMPLATE, CONVERT, CONVINCE, CORRECT, CRITICISE, CRUSH

D DARE, DEAFEN, DEFLATE, DEFY, DELIGHT, DELUDE, DEMOLISH, DENY, DEVASTATE, DEVOUR, DICTATE, DISCOURAGE, DISCOVER, DISPARAGE, DISTANCE, DISTURB, DIVERT, DOUBT

E ECHO, EDUCATE, ELEVATE, EMBARRASS, EMBITTER, EMBRACE, ENCHANT, ENCOURAGE, ENERGISE, ENFLAME, ENLIGHTEN, ENLIST, ENTERTAIN, ENTHRALL, ENTHUSE, ENTREAT, ENTRUST, EVADE, EXPOSE

F FIND, FLATTER, FLUSTER, FOCUS, FORCE, FREEZE, FRIGHTEN

G GAG, GOAD, GLORIFY, GRAB, GRIEVE, GRIND

H HARM, HARRASS, HASSLE, HOLD, HORRIFY, HUG, HUMILIATE, HUMOUR, HURRY, HURT, HUSTLE, HYPNOTISE

I IMPLORE, IMPRESS, INCITE, INFLATE, INSPIRE, INSTRUCT, INSULT, INTIMIDATE, INTRIGUE, INVIGORATE, INVITE, INVOLVE

L LEAD, LECTURE, LIGHTEN

M MANIPULATE, MENACE, MESMERISE, MOCK, MOLLIFY, MOTHER, MOVE, MYSTIFY

O OFFEND, ORGANISE, OUTBID, OVERRIDE, OVERWHELM

P PARALYSE, PATRONISE, PENETRATE, PESTER, PETRIFY, PLACATE, PLEAD, PLEASE, POISON, POKE, POLICE, POLISH, POSSESS, PRAISE, PRESSURE, PROBE, PROD, PROVOKE, PURSUE, PUSH

Q QUASH, QUELL

R RALLY, RAGE, RAPE, RAVAGE, RAVISH, REASSURE, REBUFF, REDUCE, REFUSE, REGALE, REINFORCE, REJUVENATE, RELISH, REPEL, REPRIMAND, REPROACH, REPROVE, REPUDIATE, RESCUE, RESIST, RESPECT, RESTRAIN, RESTORE, REWARD, RIDICULE, ROUSE, RUFFLE, RUSH

S SADDEN, SCALD, SCARE, SCORN, SEDUCE, SHAKE, SHAME, SHIELD, SHOCK, SILENCE, SLAP, SLOW, SNUB, SOFTEN, SOLICIT, SOOTHE, SQUASH, STAB, STAGGER, STALL, STING, STIR, STOP, STRENGHTEN, STRIKE, STROKE, SUPPORT, SURVEY, SUSPECT, SUSPEND

T TANTALISE, TEACH, TEASE, TEMPT, TEND, TERRIFY, TERRORISE, TEST, THREATEN, THRILL, TITILLATE, TOP, TORMENT, TORTURE, TRANQUILISE, TRAP, TRIP, TROUBLE, TRUMP, TWIST

U UNCOVER, UNDERCUT, UNDERMINE, UNNERVE, UPLIFT, URGE

W WARN, WELCOME, WHIP, WITHSTAND, WORRY, WORSHIP, WOUND

For a more complete list of action words with more subtle distinctions, I would suggest you buy Actions – The Actors' Thesaurus *by Marina Caldarone and Maggie Lloyd-Williams (Nick Hern Books, 2004).*

Questions in the Text

All the lines in the text that are questions should be underlined.

When someone asks a question of someone else, it is because they want an answer from them. That sounds obvious. The strange thing is that actors often choose to play questions as statements. Think about the question: 'What do you want from me?' Try saying it as an aggressive statement.

That makes sense, doesn't it? It expresses an emotion. It's realistic. And it's the way people talk.

Now try saying it as if you want to get an answer out of another person. You can even go so far as giving it an upward inflection at the end of the line. Feel as if you are not going to continue the conversation until you get an answer.

That also makes sense. It's not unrealistic and it's also the way people talk. But it also has a stronger effect on the other person because it demands an answer. Even if it doesn't get one.

Imagine that the whole line is: 'What do you want from me? Why do you give me such a bad time? What have I ever done to hurt you?'

One actor should try saying this to another actor as a list of challenging statements. It will sound truthful and it will express their character's inner turmoil. But if they try it again with the first actor asking each of these questions as if they really want a response – pausing between each question until they realise that there is not going to be an answer – they will immediately find that there is a new dynamism to the scene. And that is because the words are now communicative rather than simply being expressive. Even if the other actor doesn't respond at all, it still becomes a scene between two people because a lack of response is a response in itself.

Now, as I said, both ways of playing the lines are truthful and realistic, but what I have noticed is that actors often choose the expressive statement when they say a questioning line. They don't try to get a response. Maybe it's because lines are often learnt in isolation when there is no one around who can give them an answer even if they want one.

So I suggest that actors go through the text and make a note of all the lines that have question marks at the end of them, then they can start using them to get reactions from the other characters when they are rehearsing a scene.

All the above techniques to analyse the text are simply to try to bring life and variety to a scene in the early stages of rehearsal. In real life, people don't say anything to anyone else unless they want to have an effect on them. So the actor should find ways of using each line of dialogue in such a way that it will affect the other characters. Later on in rehearsals the specific results of all this exploration and analysis can be abandoned as the actors live truthfully in the moment.

If the actors have previously analysed the text and reflected on their objectives and actions, then whatever else happens when they are playing a scene, the unpredictable living truth they create will be underpinned by strong foundations.

8

Exits and Entrances

JAQUES. All the world's a stage,
And all the men and women merely players;
They have their exits and their entrances,
And one man in his time plays many parts…

As You Like It (2.7)

I SOMETIMES SEE ACTORS RUNNING THROUGH THEIR LINES as they wait in the wings, but that is entirely the wrong thing to do. They know their lines by now. Or they certainly should do. And they are just worrying about what's going to happen next. But actors should always let 'what's going to happen next' arrive without any predetermined expectations. They should be open, flexible and ready for anything that might occur once the scene starts. Just as in real life: we may think we know what is going to happen, but we can never be sure.

Before an actor enters a scene, they should really be thinking about what their character has been doing up until that moment. The past is the most useful preparation. The future can look after itself.

I tell actors:

'Don't think about what is going to happen, think about what has happened up until this moment.'

It's so basic and it's so important.

Starting Mid-action

Sometimes a scripted scene in a play or film starts mid-action. In other words, the characters have already been together relating to each other before the scripted scene starts. In this situation, actors should ask themselves the following questions:

- **What has happened up until this moment?**

  Sometimes, for dramatic effect, a scene will start mid-argument, so in this instance actors should ask themselves: how did the argument start? On another occasion, a scene may start just as a new character arrives. In that case, what have the other people in the scene been doing up until that moment? Did they expect the new character to arrive or are they taken by surprise? How does the interruption affect them? These questions can often be resolved through improvisation.

- **What physical activity has my character been doing?**

  Pacing the room. Doing a crossword puzzle. Eating a meal. Looking in a mirror. Anything. A physical activity will often focus an actor and bring the scene to life. When I was a young actor embarking on one of my first television jobs, a very experienced actor called Colin Douglas gave me some valuable advice: 'Always be doing something before they shout "Action!"'

- **How have the other characters affected my character's mood?**

  Whatever has happened before a scripted scene starts will have had an effect on each of the characters and put them in a certain frame of mind. One may be in a highly emotional state while another may be bored out of their mind. Maybe the emotional state is not particularly dramatic. Maybe it is not even indicated in the script because it is subtle or unspecific. But it will exist! Our moods are changing all the time.

Entering a Scene

Sometimes a character will enter in the middle of a scene. When this happens, the characters in the scripted scene will have just experienced their recent past, but the actor that enters mid-scene has to create one. In order to do that, the actor who enters the scene should ask the following questions:

- **Where has my character come from?**

  A character entering a room from a busy street will bring in an entirely different energy from someone who has just been in another room inside the house. If a character has had to dash from a taxi to the front door through the pouring rain, it will create an entirely different mood than if they have just strolled down a sunny boulevard.

- **What has my character been doing?**

  Did they have an argument with the taxi driver? Did they slip on the ice? Were they talking to an old friend they met by accident? Sometimes the script will give a clear indication of what has happened to a character before they arrive, but often nothing is mentioned. This may be because it isn't relevant to the plot, but a character's recent activity is always relevant to the actor because it will help them bring life into the scene.

- **What mood is my character in?**

  This is always important. Having decided what the character has been doing before they enter the scene, the actor should think about how this may have affected their character's mood.

- **What is my character thinking about?**

  Sometimes a character will have a strong objective in the forefront of their mind when they arrive, but on other occasions they may be thinking of something entirely inconsequential to the story. Maybe a character is wondering who will be in the room when they arrive. Or they are thinking about the weather. Or they have a problem on their mind that can't easily be resolved. It may be that none of these things has anything to do with the plot, but any of them are possible and will add another dimension to the scene.

- **Why is my character entering?**

  This might sound obvious, but it is not always clear. Especially if a character arrives on a scene by accident, as it were. Why do Abraham and Balthasar walk into 'a public place' during the opening scene of *Romeo and Juliet*? Yes, they are up for a fight when they see Sampson and Gregory, but did they know their enemies were going to be there, or were they just on their way home after a hard day's work? Were they out shopping, or were they on their way to the pub? Whatever reason they have to be there, Abraham and Balthasar will bring a certain mood or atmosphere on with them. It will be much more interesting if this mood has nothing to do with fighting, because that means everything will change the minute they see Sampson and Gregory.

- **Does my character know the room or location where the scene is taking place?**

  A familiar environment produces no surprises and is often entirely ignored, but an unfamiliar one can sometime have an impact on a character as soon as they arrive. Actors should make sure they know exactly how their character would react to the location of the scene and whether they are familiar with it or not.

- **Is my character expecting anyone to be there?**

  Walking into an empty room is entirely different from walking into a room full of people. Did the character think anyone was going to be there? Maybe there are different people in the room from those a character expected to see. These considerations will affect the character's thoughts and behaviour when they arrive.

- **Does my character know the people who are there already?**

This is similar to whether the character knows the room or location. Maybe one of the people in the room is an old friend. Or a deadly enemy. Maybe the location has several strangers in it, one of whom the character is expecting to meet, but doesn't know who it is. 'The honourable lady of the house, which is she?' says Viola in Shakespeare's *Twelfth Night* when she finds Olivia surrounded by her attendants. It's a common problem. Servants or waiters with hardly any lines could be in the room, and although they may not be referred to in the script, it may be inappropriate for the character to ignore them.

- **What is my character's attitude to each of the people that they find when they arrive?**

  This is important, especially if the character knows the other people already. Sometimes the substance of a scene overwhelms the individual relationships between the characters. But that doesn't mean they don't exist. Actors should make sure they know how their character feels about each and every person they meet. They should never generalise.

- **What does my character want as they enter a scene?**

  Objectives keep cropping up because they are the bread and butter of drama as well as of life, so actors should ask themselves what their character hopes to achieve as they enter a scene. This may change immediately depending on the circumstances, or it may change slowly, as the scene progresses. But it is important to identify a character's objective before they enter because it informs the energy and desires that the character brings on with them.

Exiting a Scene

Actors should never think that their character is leaving a scene, they should always feel that their character is going somewhere else. This will give purpose to an exit, whether it is positive or negative. Even if the character has been made to feel uncomfortable during the scene and they are storming out, the actor must know where their character is going. No one departs to nowhere. A character may not know what is going to happen next, but they should at least know what might be outside the door.

To bring an exit to life, and to understand the moment fully, actors should ask themselves the following questions:

- **Why is my character leaving?**

  This is basic and is often informed by the text. Sometimes a character makes an exit because they don't want to be there any more. Malvolio in *Twelfth Night* says: 'I'll be revenged on the whole pack of you' before he leaves, because everyone has made a fool of him and he can't wait to be out of their presence. But it is not always so obvious.

- **Where is my character going?**

  As I said, actors should never feel that their character is just leaving a scene, they have to imagine that their character is going somewhere else. Where would that be?

- **What is my character going to do next?**

  Life doesn't just stop – it carries on. An actor should decide what their character is going to do after they have left a scene. It will give their exit a reason, even if it is not outlined in the script. At the end of Act One, Scene Two in *Richard III*, Richard tells the coffin-bearers to take the body of the murdered king '…to Whitefriars, there attend my coming.' So he wants the body to go to Whitefriars, and he'll be along later, but what's he going to do with the body when he gets there? The mind boggles!

- **What mood is my character in?**

  The scene will probably have affected the character's mood, but the thought of going somewhere else may change it yet again. A character may become optimistic and positive at the thought of going somewhere else, or they may be gloomy and sad about leaving. 'Goodnight, goodnight!' says Juliet. 'Parting is such sweet sorrow, / That I shall say goodnight till it be morrow.'

- **How will my character travel to their next destination?**

  Think about it. If a limousine is waiting to whisk your character away, they will leave in an entirely different manner than they will if they have to walk to their destination, get on a horse, or search for a taxi.

- **Has my character achieved the objective they had when they first arrived?**

  If your character has achieved their objective then they will, presumably, be happy. If not, they will feel unsatisfied. Maybe their objective was abandoned as the chaos of the scene unfolded, and they only just realise this fact as they make their way out of the door. 'Dammit!' they might think. 'What a dork I am!'

~

These exits and entrances may seem trivial in the overall scheme of things, but they are important because they give the characters a life outside the scripted plot.

This places the story in the context of a wider reality, giving the audience a feeling that they are watching real people in real situations.

9
Rehearsing a Scene

BOTTOM. We will meet, and there we may rehearse most obscenely and courageously.

A Midsummer Night's Dream (1.2)

WHEN I STARTED ACTING, EACH THEATRE HAD A PERMANENT company of actors, engaged for the whole season, who would do a new play every two weeks – 'fortnightly rep' it was called – and as a result, rehearsals were quite frantic because you were rehearsing a new play during the day and performing the current play in the evenings. After opening a play on Monday evening, the company would gather on Tuesday morning to read through the next new play together and on Tuesday afternoon the director would start working through it, scene by scene, telling the actors what to do, line by line. Amazingly enough this was called 'blocking'. Think about it. A block is something that gets in the way. 'Move downstage-left when you say that line,' the director would say. Woe betide anyone who suggested that a particular move wasn't appropriate. Everything had been worked out beforehand to save time, and time was of the essence. All the actors had to do was to write these moves down and learn them along with their lines over the next few days. During this first stage of rehearsals, actors would read from their scripts as they tried the moves out. Old-school professionals would be heard to say, 'I can't learn my lines until I know my moves.'

Basically the rehearsal period was spent trying to remember the lines and the moves, and if you could get through the first night without making a mistake it was considered a great success.

Over the years, things have changed considerably!

The rehearsal process is now about research, analysis, exploration and creative artistry. The funny thing is, there is still a hangover from the old days and that is the desire that actors have to organise the shape of the play as soon as possible, and keep practising it until it runs smoothly. If there is a creative, inspirational moment during one of the rehearsals, everyone tries to hang on to it so they can do it exactly the same way next time they rehearse the scene. The trouble is, it's never quite as interesting in subsequent rehearsals, because it's not the creative moment itself. It's just a copy. Acting is exciting to watch because the audience is seeing a work of art being created before their very eyes, and if actors try to copy what they did yesterday, then the audience is only getting a reproduction of a work of art, not the original.

When actors make inspirational discoveries during the rehearsal of a scene, they shouldn't try to recreate what they did, they should try to recreate *how they felt at the moment of inspiration*. The loss of an ingenious bit of business or an unusual way of saying a line will be more than compensated for by the creative life that sparks with electricity when actors are being 'in the moment' during a performance.

Rehearsals should not be an attempt to 'get things right' and make scenes run smoothly. And performances should not be about trying to repeat things exactly the same way each night. All rehearsals and performances should be voyages of creative discovery.

Advice to Directors

Actors learn the most by being allowed to act. It's something that a lot of directors, particularly those who have never been actors, don't understand. During the early stages of rehearsal, actors are struggling with quite a few unresolved investigations, so there is a lot on their minds. Talk about multitasking! They are trying to get to grips with the creation of a character; they are getting used to the other actors; they are becoming accustomed to the overall shape of the play; they are trying to remember their lines; they are taking on board suggestions that the director might have made. Maybe they've got an unfamiliar accent to come to terms with, or a difficult fight sequence. Maybe they are trying to get their fingers around a few basic chords on a guitar or the finger-stops of a recorder. There's a lot on their minds. Directors should let them fathom it out. The biggest danger is for the director to try to get the actors to the end of the journey before they've had a chance to pack their bags. Give them time and they will work it out.

Learning the Lines

Actors can't rehearse properly until all the lines have been thoroughly learned, because they can't make the right connection with each other when they are reading from a script. So line-learning should be accomplished as soon as possible. Some actors seem to find it easier than others, but there is no trick to line-learning – it's basically just a hard slog. Having a friend or another actor reading out the other lines can make it easier. And there is an app you can get for an iPhone called Line-Learner that could be helpful. If I can give any advice, I would say that actors should always learn their lines as a response to something. That makes them easy to remember.

However quickly actors learn their lines, it is essential that they learn them accurately. Sometimes an actor will end up using their own words instead of those in the script, but this is simply diluting the personality of the character as created by the writer. There is no excuse. The lines should be accurate. It's important. As I said earlier on, writers think long and hard about which words to use. Give them the respect they deserve.

Explorative Exercises

The following exercises are useful soon after the lines have been learned. They will give the actors a chance to get used to working with each other without the pressure of trying to perform a scene.

Back to Back

The actors sit on the floor back to back with their eyes closed. They speak the words of the scene slowly, listening very carefully to each other.

This is to ensure, right from the start, that each actor is really listening to every word the other actor says. It's so easy, with all the pressure of trying to remember their own lines, for an actor to miss the subtlety and detail of what the other actor is saying. This exercise really focuses the mind so the actors listen to each other without any distractions.

Hands on the Floor

The actors sit on the floor facing each other. They each place one hand, palm down, on the floor with their fingertips touching. As they play the scene they use their hands to express their emotions: touching, caressing, drawing away, etc.

With no other distraction except the movement of their hands, the actors are able to explore the shifting emotions of their characters during a scene. They have to be responsive to each other's hand movements, and that helps them discover how they will each respond to the other actor's emotional journey.

Balancing the Stage

The actors stand facing each other as if the acting area were a large disc, balanced on a point at its centre. As the actors speak the words of the scene, they are allowed to move anywhere they like: towards each other, to the left or to the right, and away from each other. But if one actor moves forward, the other actor has to move forward as well in order to 'balance' the stage; if one moves away, the other has to move away; and if one moves to the left, they other also has to move to the left, etc.

This is to explore the shifting balance of status between the two characters. If one actor moves forward to make the scene more intimate, the other has to join in the intimacy. If the characters are quarrelling and one wants to reject the other, then they will both move apart. Each actor has to be responsive to the other actor, so neither is working in isolation. This is similar to the Hands on the Floor exercise but it takes it further. By focusing on the movements of each other, the actors are continually negotiating their positions and in that way they are able to tune in to each other. Each character has to be responsive to the other character's objectives, without losing sight of their own objectives. It's the essence of how to play a scene.

Reading In

The actors playing the scene each have a helper standing behind them with a copy of the script. The helpers read each line separately, followed by a pause as the actor thinks about how to play it. The actor then speaks the line. The helper then reads the next line, and the actor thinks of a new and interesting way to say this second line. They can say it any way they like. It shouldn't be influenced by the mood of the previous line. The helpers and the actors continue from line to line.

This exercise gives the actors time to think about what they are going to say and helps them explore different ways of communicating without the pressure of making a scene flow. They are able to take the time to give each line its own weight and importance.

In this context, a 'line' is a phrase that has a completeness of meaning. It is not necessarily a whole sentence. 'Hello, how are you? Will you be free for a meal this evening or are you doing something else?' has four phrases: 'Hello', 'how are you?', 'Will you be free for a meal tonight?', and 'or are you doing something else?' Each of these phrases should be explored in isolation.

Pause for Thought

The actors play each complete phrase separately, but before they speak it out loud, they should take a pause in order to have time to think about how they would like to express the phrase. The manner in which they choose to speak the phrase does not have to bear any relationship to the manner in which they expressed the previous phrase.

This is an extremely laborious process and it will take a long time to work through a scene, but it stops the actors from generalising the dialogue. It's like actioning the text on the hoof, but unlike that technique, where the actions are analysed and decided in isolation, the actors have to make their decisions on the spot in response to the way the other actors say their lines.

Vocalising the Subtext

The actors play the scene, but after each line they improvise the subtext out loud.

Improvising the subtext out loud will ensure that the actors are exploring their character's inner thoughts, desires and emotions. These will be changing line by line as their character engages in a conversation with another character.

Speaking the Subtext

The actors play the scene, but instead of speaking the lines in the script they just improvise the subtext.

When two actors use this exercise it enables each of them to recognise the subliminal thoughts that the other character is having. In real life, we can often sense someone else's underlying emotions and motivations when they speak to us, and obviously we respond to these subliminal messages.

Physicalising the Subtext

The actors play the scene, but, as they say the lines, they improvise physical gestures to express the subtext.

This exercise allows the text to be played at the proper speed while allowing the actors to demonstrate the subtext to each other, while continuing to explore it for themselves.

Acting the Subtext

The actors play the scene naturalistically, but allow the subtext to rise to the surface as they speak.

This is like laying the subtext on with a trowel. For instance, in Act Four of Chekhov's *Uncle Vanya*, Yelena is about to leave and is saying goodbye to Astrov, with whom she has fallen in love. Just before she goes, she takes his pencil from the table and puts it in her pocket saying, 'I'm taking this pencil as a keepsake.' Now, it's entirely reasonable for the actress playing Yelena to decide that the subtext of that line is 'I love you. I hate to leave you. And I'm taking this pencil as a lover's token which I will treasure for the rest of my life.' So when she is asked to do this exercise, she may speak the line with all the passion of a lover, kissing the pencil and holding it to her breast, as she sighs and looks lovingly into Astrov's eyes. This is allowing the subtext to rise to the surface and it is entirely non-realistic, but it helps the actors to understand the depth of thought or emotion that their character is trying to hide.

Actors often think that subtext should be used like this – or perhaps a diluted version of my example – but by definition subtext is the unexpressed thoughts and emotions beneath the surface of the dialogue. and it should be kept that way.

The previous four exercises allow the actor to think about the subtext; explore the subtext; demonstrate the subtext; and play the subtext, but they are all leading to this final exercise.

Thinking the Subtext

The actors play the scene naturalistically, but they continually think about the subtext without any form of demonstration.

This exercise brings the use of subtext closer to reality. In real life, we often try to keep our thoughts and emotions hidden as we speak. So in the example from *Uncle Vanya* above, Yelena would think about how passionately she loves Astrov as she says the line, but at the same time she would try to keep all that passion hidden as she simply tells him that she is going to keep his pencil as a keepsake. When actors are doing this exercise they should keep focused on the subtext, but never allow it to show.

Finally, of course, the actors will play the scene as it is written and the subtext will be imbedded into their psyche, just as it is in real life. What is affecting for an audience is when they can sense that there is something going on beneath the surface. When actors overplay the subtext, they are underestimating the power of the audience's psychological radar, and as a result the audience doesn't get so involved because it is being spoon-fed. But if the audience is allowed to detect extremely understated 'messages' for itself, it will feel as if it is part of the process. This is audience participation on an extremely subtle level.

I can't let this go without flagging it up in a simple phrase:

Actors should keep the subtext 'sub'.

Gobbledegook

The actors play the whole scene, line by line, using gobbledegook instead of the text.

Gobbledegook is a made-up language that doesn't actually mean anything. (Some actors find it hard to speak gobbledegook, so as an alternative they can recite the days of the week or the colours of the rainbow.) The exercise will ensure that the actors are really trying to communicate with each other. It also helps them to understand the rhythms, moods and shifting relationships that happen during the scene.

Gobbledegook sometimes sounds Italian or Russian, and there is a danger that the actors might start playing cultural stereotypes. Or they might start trying to be funny. If either of these things happen, it's important to remind them that the exercise is a serious exploration of how the characters communicate with each other.

Mime

The actors play the whole scene in mime instead of using any words at all.

This has a similar effect to using gobbledegook, but it is particularly useful for actors who like to express themselves physically. It will give all actors in the scene a clear understanding of their shared responsibility.

Whispering

The actors play the scene whispering the text to each other, but without necessarily standing close to each other.

This exercise is beneficial for several reasons. Firstly, the actors have to make sure they are communicating the sense of the dialogue with clarity and articulation; and secondly, each actor has to concentrate on what the other actors are saying in case they miss anything.

This exercise also has an impact on the urgency and dynamism of a scene, because the actors have to be fully focused on each other.

Blindfold

The actors play the scene with blindfolds on.

This is obviously more useful in a scene that doesn't have too much physical action, otherwise it becomes an exercise in stumbling around, trying not to bump into anything. It works best in a scene where the actors are either sitting down or standing quite still.

The exercise is about listening. Without any visual distractions, the actors listen to the words more carefully and concentrate on each other more fully.

It's also useful to prevent the actors from using excessive hand gestures to emphasise certain lines of dialogue. If there is no point in using gestures because no one can see them, the actors will start to use the words more emphatically to put their meaning across.

Double-time

The actors play the scene at twice the normal speed, but without losing the truth, the objectives or the desire to communicate their character's thoughts to the other characters.

This exercise will sharpen the actors' thoughts and ensure that they are pausing for the right reasons. Some actors use 'dramatic pauses' in rehearsal to give them time to remember their lines, but they should be so on top of the dialogue that they can speak it without having to search for the next line. This exercise will throw up any weaknesses in the actor's memory.

But there is more to it than that. A double-speed run will sometimes bring a scene to life and make everyone realise that they have been rather indulgently slow. Some actors take too much time reacting to what another character has said and thinking about how they feel, before they speak their next line. Apart from making a scene incredibly slow, it is not actually what people do in real life. People usually speak as they think, letting the words express their immediate thoughts.

Actors should make their characters think and speak at the same time.

Variety of Styles

The actors play the scene in a different theatrical or cinematic style, e.g.

Agitprop (political theatre)
American musical
Commedia dell'Arte
Costume drama
Epic theatre (Brecht)
Fairytale
Farce
Gothic horror
Grand opera
Greek tragedy
Hollywood Golden Age
Mills & Boon romance
Modern fantasy
Physical theatre
Reality TV (*Big Brother*)
Silent film
Soap opera
Spaghetti Western
The Matrix
The Simpsons
Theatre of the Absurd
Trainspotting
Victorian melodrama

These variations can only be used once the actors can run a scene with confidence.

By exploring the nature of a scene in unexpected ways, the actors learn to jettison preconceived notions and ideas. It's hard to be specific because every case is different, but discoveries are often made which would never have been revealed in normal circumstances.

This exercise can sometimes be used to add a particular flavour or mood to a scene – by choosing a genre which is an exaggerated version of something that lies buried within the scene that the actors are struggling to express. For instance, when Sampson and Gregory confront Abraham and Balthasar in the first scene of *Romeo and Juliet*, they may be finding it hard to capture the right mood. So they could try playing it in the style of a Spaghetti Western to see if that brings out the tension of the scene. Or they could try is as a farce to see if that will reveal the characters' sense of humour.

Points of Concentration

Each actor is given (or chooses) one aspect of their character's thoughts, feelings or desires to concentrate on fully while they run a whole scene. Then they take another aspect and run the

scene again. This can be done several times. Each time is a 'point of concentration'.

This exercise explores the complex layers of subtextual thought and mood within a scene by concentrating on each in isolation. For instance, during a scene a character may feel all of the following:

- A desire to be powerful
- Love for the other person in the scene
- The need to leave as soon as possible
- Sick

So, by running the scene four times, concentrating on one of these at a time, the layers of subtext build upon each other. You can, of course, choose your own 'points of concentration' depending on the nature of the scene.

A good example is the opening speech from *Richard III* which starts 'Now is the winter of our discontent / Made glorious summer by this son of York.'

During this speech Richard is feeling all of the following:

- Ugly and unattractive to women
- Hated by everybody
- Bored because the war is over
- Ambitious to become king
- Overconfident that he will achieve his ambition
- Fearful of failure
- In a hurry to get what he wants

I'm sure that any actor playing the part will agree with most of these. Maybe they will even want to add more. But it can be very difficult to think of all these complex emotions and desires at the same time. In real life, they would be embedded in Richard's psyche and he wouldn't have to think about them, but an actor has to find each of these for himself. It would be useful to run through the speech seven times, each time concentrating solely on one of the bullet points above. This will help the actor build the many emotions, ambitions and fears that Richard is experiencing at the beginning of the play.

Playing a scene with a specific point of concentration can also be used later in rehearsals if an actor is having difficulty feeling or expressing some specific aspect of their character. For instance, in Act Two, Scene One of *Hamlet*, Ophelia comes to tell her father Polonius that Hamlet has been behaving in a very strange way. If the actress is having trouble feeling the shock of the experience as she relates it to her father, her point of concentration could be the look that Hamlet gave her as he walked out of the door, or even a mental picture of Hamlet in a straitjacket being locked in a padded cell.

Listening and Responding

When actors are rehearsing a scene or reading a script with the rest of the cast, they should listen to what the other characters are saying and how they are saying it. And then they should let their own lines be a response to what they have heard.

It sounds obvious, but this is vitally important. Actors are often so concerned about their own character and their own character's objectives that they only half-listen to the other actors. They need to make sure that what they say is always a response to what they hear. There is more about this in Chapters 11 and 12, but it is so crucial for truthful acting that I need to flag it up now.

Actors should always listen to the other actors, and their lines should be a response to what they hear.

Thinking

Actors should make sure they are always thinking within the scene, even when they have nothing to say.

Yet again, this might sound obvious, but it's not as easy as it seems. It requires a lot of concentration and is particularly important when an actor is in front of a camera. But don't misunderstand this. Actors shouldn't fall into the trap of *demonstrating* their characters' thoughts. That is not what I mean at all. All the actor has to do is to think the right thoughts for their character, be present, and *stay in the moment.*

Rehearsals are the opportunity for actors to make wild experiments and to try out extraordinary ideas. There should be no fear of failure because there is nothing to fail. Everything should be about learning and discovery. My advice is to keep making adventurous choices, and not give up if they don't seem to work. They can always be tried again from a different perspective. It's only in the last few days of rehearsal that an unsuccessful choice needs to be abandoned.

Rehearsals are not there to polish a rough diamond: they are there to cut the jewel into a myriad of colourful facets.

10
Rehearsal Improvisations

> SIR TOBY. It is no matter how witty, so it be eloquent and full of invention.
>
> *Twelfth Night* (3.2)

USING IMPROVISATION AS PART OF THE REHEARSAL PROCESS is a massively helpful tool because it combines the actors' creative imagination with their talent to pretend to be other people. When actors make improvisations around a text, they allow their instincts and their own personal experience to be the 'search engines' for making new discoveries. Improvisation as part of an actor's creative process is what Google is to the internet. It makes it so much easier to find what you're looking for. And more.

But rehearsal improvisations have to be handled carefully for them to be of any use. In order to learn something about their characters, or any other aspect of the script, the improvisations have to be truthful, personal explorations based in a realistic world. And the actors should embark on the improvisation without any preconceived ideas, and just see what happens.

In order for them to be able to do that, the improvisation needs to have firm foundations. It's like building a house. In order to make it stable and functional, you need a ground plan; you need solid foundations; you need high-quality materials; and you need an extensive toolbox.

Building a Structured Improvisation

Ground Plan

Before the actors start an improvisation they should make sure they all agree about certain basic facts.

Some of these facts will be uncovered during the analysis of the text and some will be discovered during the research process. Some facts will also have been created by the actors as they build their characters, and others will emerge from the exploratory rehearsal exercises. There may also be additional facts dictated by the set and costume designers, as well as conceptual facts that are determined by the director's vision of the play as a whole.

- **The given circumstances**

  The given circumstances are the undisputed facts that are written into the script. *Romeo and Juliet* is set in Verona. It says so in the opening lines. As the play starts, Romeo is in love with Rosaline (at least he thinks he is); Juliet is thirteen years old; and the Montagues and the Capulets are bitter enemies. All this is written into the script. They are unarguable facts. A group discussion will unearth as many given circumstances as possible.

- **Research**

  Research information is very important when embarking on rehearsal improvisations, particularly if the action of the piece takes place in another era or another culture. The actors may not be wearing costumes during rehearsals, but it is important for them to know what clothes their character would be wearing. Similarly, it's important to know the cultural etiquette of the world in which the production is set. Each actor's research material can be shared with the group, so everyone understands as much as they can about the world in which the improvisation is to be set.

- **The situation**

  Before a rehearsal improvisation starts, all the actors involved should be clear about the situation or scenario that they are about to improvise. Having said that, it can sometimes be useful to withhold certain bits of information from some of the actors, so they can discover how they character would react without any preconceived ideas. For instance, if Hamlet and his mother Gertrude were improvising a scene in her bedroom, just after Hamlet's father had died, it would be quite interesting to discover what Hamlet's reaction would be if Claudius suddenly emerged from an en suite bathroom with a towel wrapped around his waist. If the actor playing Hamlet hadn't been told this in advance and he stayed totally committed to the improvisation, then his own reaction could give him an insight into how Hamlet feels about Claudius at the beginning of the play. But this is an add-on to the basic facts about the situation and it has a specific purpose. Generally speaking, information doesn't need to be withheld from the actors. They should all know as much as they can about the scenario. (There is a more detailed description of this and many other improvisation techniques in my book *Improvisation in Rehearsal*, also published by Nick Hern Books.)

- **Who are you supposed to be?**

It's important that actors knows as much as possible about the characters that they are taking into an improvisation. This may sound obvious, but sometimes a rehearsal improvisation may be set several years before the action of the play, when the characters were teenagers rather than the jaded married couple they have become. On another occasion, the actors may be improvising characters that are not actually in the script. Romeo is in love with Rosaline at the beginning of *Romeo and Juliet*, but she never actually appears in the play, so it could be useful for Romeo to improvise a scene with an actress taking on the role of Rosaline. This could help him discover the difference between Romeo's normal feelings of romance compared to the ecstatic feelings he has when he meets Juliet. The actress taking on this role obviously wouldn't know a lot about Rosaline, so a discussion with the group beforehand could help her to establish a fully rounded character. This will help to make the improvisation seem more realistic for the actor playing Romeo.

- **Who are all the other actors in an improvisation supposed to be?**

  Sometimes a rehearsal improvisation may involve a whole group of actors taking on roles that are not in the script. For instance, in Act Three, Scene Two of Shakespeare's *Julius Caesar*, there is a crowd of Plebeians in the Forum, several of which have specific lines, but a lot of others that don't. In order to make the scene come to life, a group improvisation could be set up to allow the actors to improvise their reactions to Brutus and Mark Antony without any inhibitions. But before the improvisation starts, each actor should make sure they know who all the other actors are supposed to be and what the relationships are amongst the group, if any.

- **Where does the improvisation take place?**

  It's no good starting a rehearsal improvisation if the actors aren't clear about where it's taking place. If necessary, the group can prepare a 'set' beforehand and talk it through. It doesn't have to be sophisticated. A room can be mapped out in a rehearsal space with chairs representing sofas, beds, walls, etc. There could be a door to the kitchen at one corner and a door to the rest of the house at another. It can also be useful to have a discussion about the atmosphere of the room. The colour and the texture of furnishings. The ambient sounds. The lingering aroma of cigarettes, perfume or cooking. If the room is owned by one of the characters in the improvisation, it will be useful for the actor playing that part to describe these details to the other actors involved. Most of the time there will be no actual set, but if all the actors agree about the details, they will be able to imagine their environment more vividly as they improvise.

- **What has your character been doing?**

  Each of the actors in an improvisation needs to think about what their character has actually been doing up until the moment the improvisation begins. Where have they come from and how did they get here? Who have they been with? What were they up to? And so on.

- **How is your character feeling?**

  Each actor should think about the emotion their character feels just before the improvisation takes place – and what caused it. This may not have anything to do with the improvisation scenario that the actors are about to embark on, but no situation in real life starts with a blank canvas. Our emotional state is always affected by what has recently happened, and the actors should bring that emotional state into the improvisation as they start.

- **The finer details**

  What is the weather like? How is everyone dressed? When did the characters last meet? What time of day is it? What time of year? Etc. Etc. These finer details should only be discussed if they are relevant to the scenario, otherwise there would be no end to the discussion and the improvisation would never start.

Foundations

Rehearsal improvisations should always be truthful, no matter how extreme the situation may be.

The Truth

The cornerstone of any rehearsal improvisation is reality itself. If the actors create a realistic improvisation they will make honest discoveries about their characters, the situation and the relationships that exist in the play. It's as simple as that.

The Objectives

In order to support the reality that they are trying to create, the actors should give their characters clear objectives.

- **What does my character want?**
- **Why is my character here?**
- **Why has my character decided to have a conversation?**

These objectives should be decided before the improvisation begins, but the way that a character achieves his or her objectives should be discovered during the improvisation itself. This will depend on the way the other characters in the improvisation behave, what they say and how they say it. Actors should let their characters be in the moment, so they can react and respond organically, and use appropriate tactics to achieve their objectives. It may be useful to decide on a tactic for achieving an objective, but it's much more revealing to discover how to achieve that objective through improvisation.

Building Materials

The Mind

During an improvisation, the actors should be alert to whatever is happening around them and then respond instinctively to whatever they see and hear. They should let their imagination flow – uninhibited, unbound and without reservations.

- **The most important building material is the actor's *imagination*.**
- **They should keep their *ears* open and react to whatever they hear.**
- **They should keep their *eyes* open and react to whatever they see.**
- **They should keep their *mind* open and react to whatever happens.**

The important thing to remember during an improvisation is that self-censorship can be death to the imagination. It doesn't matter if an improvisation appears to be going 'wrong' because any wild deviations from the straight and narrow can always be discussed and eliminated after it has finished. A total commitment to the improvisation is essential while it is taking place. It's an experiment that the actors undertake in order to make discoveries. If the experiment doesn't unfold the way the actors imagined it would, then they are already learning something. Things are revealed that would never have been discovered by any other means. But if actors censor their improvisations and stop them before they have properly got under way, they may miss out on important discoveries.

Actors should also be prepared to ignore any small errors that may occur during an improvisation. A particular piece of information in the script may have been missed, or a fact forgotten, which may be referred to incorrectly by one of the actors. But like self-censorship, it is much more important to allow the improvisation to flow, than to stop it in order to point out a mistake. The finer details can easily be discussed after the improvisation has finished.

The Body

During a rehearsal improvisation, actors can create the world around them without needing anything other than their own physicality.

- **They can use their *body* to create the physical world they inhabit.**
- **They can use realistic *mime skills* to create any props, settings and/or costumes that the scene requires.**

Miming things that aren't there should not become an end in itself, but it is an extremely useful way for the actors to create the physical world that their characters inhabit, and mimed props don't need anything except the actor's imagination.

An Improviser's Toolbox

Being There

Whoever the actors are supposed to be, whatever situation their characters are in and wherever the location, all the actors have to do is behave however they feel their characters would behave. The actors shouldn't feel they need to make their characters say or do anything. All they have to do is 'be there' and see what happens.

Above all, the actors should never try to entertain or impress anyone else. These rehearsal improvisations are for the actors' own explorations and have no other purpose.

Atmosphere

The actors should create the atmosphere of the improvised location by the way they use their voices, move around and interact with the other characters. This helps everyone feel the 'truth' of the scenario.

Activities

The actors should think about a physical activity that their character could be doing in the improvisation. This will help to channel the focus of their attention, and it will often bring about the natural rhythms of a conversation. Maybe a character is playing solitaire with a pack of cards, while the other is cleaning the room. Maybe they are both keeping a lookout in case anyone can overhear. Maybe they are even playing a game of squash as they speak, or simply eating a meal. A physical activity will help the actors create a truthful environment in which to place their characters.

Character

In the early stages of rehearsal, it is common for actors to use stereotypical characters when they are improvising and adopt vocal and physical characteristics unlike their own. But that is something to be avoided because it is ultimately very limiting. (Some of the work on characters as described in Chapter 5 will give the actor a suitable starting point.) The actors should never try to push a characterisation too far in the early stages. They should let their character grow during the improvisations by attempting to 'get inside the character's head'.

Actors should try to *think* like their characters, not *act* like them.

Listening

It's common for actors to feel anxious about improvising because they fear they won't have anything to say. Some actors overcompensate and gabble away about anything, while others just clam up, but if the actors simply listen carefully to each other, they will find plenty to feed the conversation. Listening is vital during an improvisation, because it paves the way for imaginative dialogue. There are various ways to help an actor focus on what another actor is saying during an improvisation, but the simplest way is to listen out for a phrase or an idea that could take the conversation in a new direction.

Responding

The biggest mistake during a rehearsal improvisation is to shy away from risky dialogue. Often actors give a safe response to a question so they won't get taken down unprepared paths. For instance, I often hear something along the lines of the following:

ACTOR ONE. Hi! What have you been up to?

ACTOR TWO. Nothing much.

Or:

ACTOR ONE. Do you have any brothers and sisters?

ACTOR TWO. No.

Both of these are naturalistic responses, so it is ridiculous to say that they don't seem to be real. But these choices are too safe because nothing is being explored. And if nothing is explored, nothing will be discovered. The risky, but more creative response to the first question, 'What have you been up to?', would be to say something like: 'Well, I just got sacked from my job yesterday because I was late too often.' Or 'I went down to Brighton at the weekend with two old friends from school and we all swam in the sea.' Both of these responses take the improvisation into uncharted territory. What was the job? Why were you late? What old friends? Was the sea cold? And that means that the actor will have to start making things up on the spot.

And that's when an improvisation gets creative.

But to take it further, how does Actor One respond to Actor Two's response?

ACTOR ONE. Hi! What have you been up to?

ACTOR TWO. Well, I got sacked from my job yesterday because I was late too often.

It's tempting for Actor One to say, 'Oh no. Tell me about it,' but that is merely throwing the ball back into the other actor's court. A much better response from Actor One would be to say something like 'You're lucky, I haven't had a job since I broke my leg last spring.'

Then, in three lines of dialogue an enormous amount of information has been added to the improvisation. A sacking. Lateness. Unemployment. A broken leg. Where could all this lead?

The answer is that it could lead anywhere, but at least it will be an interesting journey.

There are several methods of making creative dialogue, and they all start with listening to the other actor and making imaginative responses to what is being said.

- **Creating a history:** This is when something that Actor One says inspires Actor Two to make up a story about their character's life.

  ACTOR ONE. Shall we go to the fair?

  ACTOR TWO. Hey, I'll tell you something. I went to a fair when I was fifteen, and I met this guy who was operating the dodgem cars. He took me back to his place, and I met his wife, who had just got back from India...

  And so on. There is the danger that Actor Two will just keep talking, but if Actor One is really listening, he or she can interrupt at any time. For instance, Actor One could pick up on the word 'India' and say something like: 'It's funny you should mention India because a whole family from Mumbai have just moved in next door to my mother. She went in to see if they needed anything but...' And so on.

- **Confirming the details:** This is when the second actor recognises something that the first actor mentions and expands on it.

  ACTOR ONE. I went to a party on Saturday night.

  ACTOR TWO. Oh, do you meant that party where a fight broke out between Dave and Boris and the police arrived to break the whole thing up?

- **Being an expert:** This is when the first actor mentions something and the second actor behaves as if he or she were an expert on that particular subject.

  ACTOR ONE. It's a nice day.

  ACTOR TWO. Yeah, but did you know that a sunny day following two days of rain will draw the moisture out of the damp earth to create a fine mist. If it's sunny before ten in the morning, the mist will disperse some time in the middle of the afternoon, otherwise it will linger till sunset.

> This is, of course, rubbish, and I improvised it as I was writing to demonstrate the point. These ideas don't have to be true, because the actor isn't really an expert on the subject, but if he or she can make their character behave like an expert it can make the dialogue more interesting.

The important thing is to listen, respond, and make up stories. It's the lifeblood of dynamic improvisations.

Of course, this kind of creative dialogue takes a lot of practice before the actors are fully confident, but once they get the hang of it, they will be liberated by their own imagination and spontaneity.

Feeding

While actors can be listening out for something to stimulate their improvised dialogue, they can also feed each other with new ideas. For instance, one actor could say: 'I heard your brother just got married.' This throws the ball into the other actor's court, because they may not have even considered whether their character has any brothers and sisters. The second actor will have to think on the spot and make something up; otherwise the improvisation won't make any sense. 'Yes, it's about time. He's been engaged for six years, but wanted to wait till they could afford a down-payment on a flat.' And then a life is created, as the actor builds a family background for their character.

Re-incorporating

Another way the actors can find fuel for their creativity is to think back over everything that has happened since the improvisation started. They can then refer to something that was mentioned earlier in the conversation and chat about it some more. This exploration of the details will ensure that the improvisation doesn't get too diluted by the continual addition of new ideas.

Building Together

It's important for actors to remember that they are never alone in an improvisation, and no one has total responsibility for making the scenario work. They can help each other out. All they have to do is be there, listen and respond, and feed off each other.

Personal Incident

At any point during an improvisation, one of the actors can create a personal incident, like a nosebleed, hiccups or something in the eye. This will take the mood of an improvisation into a new direction, without losing sight of the main theme. It's very easy to think that an actor is 'spoiling' an improvisation if they change the mood, but really they are expanding it and making it come alive. Actors should always be open to each other's moments of creativity.

External Incident

This is a similar idea to the personal incident, and it can be used for the same reasons. The difference lies in the fact that the actor has to make the incident something external to themselves, like the roof leaking, or a blackout, or an earthquake. These incidents can be quite dramatic, but they should remain within the reality of the scene. It would be beyond the realm of credibility if two people were improvising a scene in a small flat in West London, and one of them said, 'Oh my God! It's a flash flood!'

When an actor is creating an external incident, they must always make sure that the other actor knows exactly what is supposed to be happening. If one actor looks horrified and says, 'Oh no! Look at that! What are we going to do?', the other actor will have no idea what the first actor had in mind. It would be better to say, 'Oh no! Look at the smoke pouring out of that upstairs window! What are we going to do?'

Of course, if the first actor has said, 'Oh no! Look at that! What are we going to do?', the second actor can always make something up: 'It's a terrible car crash. We should go and see if they need help.' When this happens, the first actor has to abandon his original unspoken idea and just go with the new one. It would obviously be pointless to say, 'It isn't a car crash, it's smoke pouring from an upstairs window,' because then one character or the other would appear to be insane.

Extreme Incident

Again, this is similar to the incidents described above, but takes the idea further and should only be used if it is appropriate. These would be extreme incidents like a ghost appearing, or aliens landing, or someone being possessed by the devil or turning into a werewolf. Actors have to have a lot of trust in each other to make extreme incidents truthful, but incidents like this often happen in films, and actors have to learn how to respond to them with a truthful commitment.

Blocking

In the context of improvisation, blocking is when someone says something and the other person denies it. For instance, if one actor says, 'It's raining,' and the other says, 'No, it's not, the sun is shining,' then the second actor is blocking because it can't be both. One actor might say, 'Hello Mum,' and if the other actor says, 'I'm not your Mum, I'm your sister,' then they too are blocking. Once one actor establishes something, then the other actor has to go with that idea, even if it means abandoning something fabulously interesting that they were just about to say.

Adjusting the Scenario

Actors should never be afraid of adjusting a scenario, as long as they remain faithful to the given circumstances. It can be useful to make the description of the scenario reasonably minimal in order to give the actors plenty of room to manoeuvre. For instance, the director might suggest that the actors explore their characters' relationship by doing an improvisation in which they meet for a drink in a bar. That is the scenario, and they could just start the improvisation. But before they start, one of the actors could decide that he has already been drinking before the meeting takes place, or the other might decide that he has just come from a successful job interview. Either of these ideas would give the improvisation a particular quality even if they were not what the director had in mind, but neither of them would be unfaithful to the original scenario, so they would be quite acceptable. That way, both the actors and the director will be learning from each other.

Be Anarchic

Actors should have the courage to make bold choices during an improvisation. They should never be trying to please the director; they should be trying to give the director something unexpected and original.

But whatever anarchic decisions an actor may make during an improvisation, they should always find the truth of the situation, however extreme they make it.

Welcome Anarchy

No matter how much the anarchic imagination of one actor affects an improvisation, the other actors should welcome the changes with open arms and go with the flow.

And then they should be anarchic back!

Some of the techniques described in this chapter are straightforward and, providing the actors keep within the truth of the improvisation, they can be used in the rehearsals of any play or film. But others need to be practised in order for the actors to use them with confidence. As soon as an improvisation gets dangerously unpredictable, inexperienced actors will often lose focus and either give up or start to laugh. So extreme choices should be used with caution.

But improvisation is a fabulous tool and its dynamic and creative possibilities are often underestimated.

11

Meisner Training

Why with the time do I not glance aside
To new-found methods and to compounds strange?

Sonnet LXXVI

EACH GENERATION OF ACTING TUTORS REFINES THE techniques of the previous generation in order to suit the climate of the times. Each decade seems to have its own particular version of naturalism, as can be seen by looking at old films. But the interesting thing is that the performances that have stood the test of time still look truthful today, whatever style of acting is going on around them. As a young actor, I was taught to use my voice with articulation and modulation in order to ensure that the audience could understand what I was saying. The acting style in current television drama is to whisper lines so intensely that they can hardly be heard. But whatever the prevailing trend, the actors who we all remember are the ones who live truthfully through their performance.

John Wayne has starred in more films than anyone else, and his record is unlikely to be broken. When I was young, I rather looked down on John Wayne because I didn't think he was a 'real' actor. In fact, he didn't even seem to take himself seriously as an actor. He famously said: 'I don't act… I react.' And it's true. Look at his films now, even ones that were made seventy or eighty years ago, and he still looks alive on the screen. There is nothing spectacular about the way he phrases his lines, and the dialogue doesn't even seem that important to him. But watch his eyes. See him listen. Watch him respond. It's thrilling. If you ask yourself why John Wayne starred in more films than anyone else, you have to say that it is because people wanted to watch him on the screen. And what they wanted to watch was the life he brought to his performances. Each of his films was so truthful it was like seeing a documentary about the life of John Wayne. Indeed, in his early Westerns his character was often actually called John! And at least three of the characters he played in the late 1930s and early 1940s were called Duke, which eventually became his nickname.

'An ounce of behaviour is worth more than a pound of words.' (Sanford Meisner)

I've no idea whether the American acting guru Sanford Meisner appreciated the acting style of John Wayne, but there is no doubt that they both believed in some of the same things. Stanislavsky was right in asking actors to look inside themselves to find the truth of the character, but by the time his training had been imported to America and refined by Lee Strasberg, Stella Adler and the Group Theatre in the middle of the last century, 'The Method', as it came to be called, had become a cult of the inner life of a character. But Meisner thought this was putting the actors inside their heads too much. Their focus was exclusively on themselves, and as a result their performances seemed to be too inward-looking. His idea was simply to develop some exercises to train the actor to get their attention off themselves and onto the other actor. He thought that all good acting was reactive and that an impulsive response could be trained and strengthened like a muscle. If you pinch someone, they say 'ouch'. But they can't say 'ouch' until they've been pinched. And what is also important to remember is that the 'ouch' response happens impulsively, before they've even had time to think about it.

Meisner came up with an exercise called *repetition* in order to help the actor to see clearly, and respond truthfully and impulsively from their own point of view. He said repetition was like a ballet exercise, which trains the muscles of seeing clearly and responding truthfully so the response becomes habitual. It's like the two blades of a pair of self-sharpening scissors. The more they are used, the sharper they get.

Once the actors have strengthened these muscles, then they can add the given circumstances to bring a scene to life.

What follows is a series of exercises and rehearsal techniques that we teach to the second-year acting students at ArtsEd. Although they are based on Meisner techniques and inspired by them, they are not necessarily pure Meisner. Aileen Gonsalves, who teaches these techniques, continues to develop and refine them to suit the needs of the modern actor. The Meisner training is a big step for our students to take for two reasons. Firstly, they have been taught how to analyse a text in order to bring the dialogue to life, yet Meisner trains them to do the same thing by trusting their own instincts in performance. And secondly, they have been shown how to create character through research and physical transformation, yet Meisner says that 'character' is the actor him or herself under a given set of circumstances.

Actually, these approaches are not mutually exclusive. Both are trying to achieve the same thing: i.e. a truthful performance and an expressive characterisation. But where one approach does this analytically in the rehearsal room the other does it impulsively during an actual performance. It's like learning to drive a car. At first you have to concentrate on how to operate the steering wheel, the brakes and the gear shift, but once you have learned the technique it becomes more and more instinctive, until eventually you forget all about it, concentrate on the journey, and respond to whatever is happening around you.

Meisner ensures that truthful creativity happens in performance and not just in rehearsal. As I said before:

Performance should be a reflection of life, not a reproduction of it.

The Reality of Doing

The actors count the number of books on a shelf, or they listen for the number of cars passing outside the window.

This exercise introduces the actors to the concept of being unaffectedly real even when they are being observed.

The simple activity of counting books on a shelf is easy to do. If all the actors do it together and are then asked to say how many books they have counted, they will tell you straight out: 'Twelve!' – because that is the truth. It's simple.

But if half of the group are told to go and count the books while the other half watches, some of them will start 'acting' counting the books because they feel they have to do something. But they don't. They have to learn to trust the truth of the activity. All they need to do is literally count the books on the shelf and find out how many there are.

It's the same when the actors are asked to listen and respond. They don't have to 'act' listening or 'act' responding; they just have to listen and then let the response happen by itself.

The only thing that makes this simple activity difficult is the actors' desire to get it right and to be good at it. And that only comes about because they are being observed. In real life, no one thinks twice about whether they are listening correctly, or being good at responding to something. They just do it.

Acting is the reality of doing.

Observing the World

The actors walk around the room, tuning in to everything that they can see, hear and smell.

There is so much that we ignore going on in the world around us. In fact, we learn how to filter our sensory input from a very early age to make it possible to function. Of course, it's important to hear a car coming down the road, otherwise we might get run over, but when we are indoors we soon learn to ignore the sound of traffic outside the window because it poses no danger. We walk down a crowded street surrounded by all manner of people who pass us by in a blur because our brain filters out anything that doesn't interest us – but if there is an attractive person coming towards us we notice them immediately. Just because our attention is drawn towards a particularly bad smell or a particularly sweet perfume, it doesn't mean that our noses aren't working the rest of the time.

Unfortunately, when we are acting, this filtering of our sensory input often works against us because we filter out the wrong things. It's important to remember the lines or to monitor our objectives and actions, but this inward-thinking can cause us to filter out the subtle changes of thought and emotion that are being expressed by the people we are acting with. We don't listen to them properly because we already know what they are saying. It's the same thing they said last time we ran the scene. It's the words of the script.

But if actors practise observing every detail of the room they will become accustomed to taking the attention off themselves and putting it onto something external. Ultimately, this will include the other actors and the scene they are in.

Responding

Without talking, two actors walk back and forth towards each other, each responding to the other's movements.

As they do this, each person should only move if the other person makes them want to move. They shouldn't be generous by trying to make it easy for the other person, they should simply let themselves respond impulsively. If they don't want to walk back just because the other person is walking back, then they don't have to do it. The actors have to understand that they have permission to make an uninhibited response without self-censorship.

They shouldn't try to 'get it right'.

This exercise encapsulates the whole Meisner technique, so it is worth monitoring what the actors are doing in order for them to understand the very basics. Some people will want to please their opposite number and bring harmony to the exercise by mirroring everything they do, while others will be constantly opposing their partner's moves as they try to take control. Some people will try to be funny; others will try to be clever. This is because they are trying to 'do something' rather than allowing themselves to be instinctive. In order to avoid this danger, it is useful for the actors to maintain eye contact, and avoid talking or touching.

By practising this exercise, the actors learn to tune in to the subtleties of each other's behaviour and make instinctive responses.

Repetition

Repetition is the primary tool of Meisner training, and it needs to be taught carefully so that the actors will be able to use it without thinking. It can seem strange at first, and learning how to do it takes up a lot of time. Several sessions at least. But then practising the scales on a piano can seem strange when all you want to do is play a piano concerto. And practising piano scales certainly takes up a lot of time.

Stage One

Two actors sit in chairs facing each other, about one to two metres apart, while the rest of the group watches. One of the actors starts by simply observing some behaviour in the other person. For instance, they might say, 'You're crossing your arms.' The other actor then repeats that sentence word for word: 'You're crossing your arms.' Then they both keep repeating the same sentence word for word, taking it in turns.

Of course, this doesn't make any sense at all, but that doesn't matter at this stage because the actors are trying to get to the pure emotion that exists beneath the surface of the words. Meisner thought that language was like a canoe that floats on the surface of the river of emotions. So the words in this exercise are simply a conduit for the actors to connect with each other. They don't have to do anything except to listen and repeat the words exactly. But the way they say the words – the quality or emotional content – must be an unconscious, truthful response to how the other actor makes them feel. Each actor's attention must always be on the other actor.

When they first do this exercise they may find themselves thinking about how they should respond. This is because their focus is within themselves. In their own heads. What we are trying to do is to get their focus away from themselves and onto someone else, so they can respond without thinking. They need to get out of their heads. It's like Luke Skywalker in *Star Wars* when he learns to 'feel the force'. They have to let go of their desire to be in control.

As the actors play around with this exercise, they have to be continually reminded to get out of their own heads. When the exercise is done properly it can be very exposing, because each actor's attention is entirely on the other actor, and that means their defences are down. This is exactly what happens when you fall in love. You are purely focused on the other person, and you are really seeing them. And if the object of your desire is in love with you, then they are really seeing you. Love is not about two individuals; it's about the moment when two people connect with each other. It's the reality and the honesty of that moment that we are trying to achieve as actors.

The emotions that come to the surface during repetition are not always romantic or joyful. Sometimes they can be aggressive and confrontational, so there is one major rule for these Meisner exercises:

No one is allowed to hit anyone.

Stage Two

Two actors stand up and face each other. As before, one of them starts by observing some behaviour in the other person. But this time the pronoun changes in response to the other actor. For instance, if one person says, 'You're crossing your arms,' then the other says, 'I'm crossing my arms.' The first person continues with, 'You're crossing your arms,' and the other responds with, 'I'm crossing my arms.' And so on.

This slight shift starts to give some meaning to the dialogue, and this makes the actors want to be inventive with their emotional response. As a result, they tend to go back into their heads and start 'acting'. This can be closely monitored by reminding them to get out of their heads. In other words, they should put their attention totally on the other person and let their responses be as impulsive as before. They are trying to achieve an emotional response without thinking about it or 'doing' anything.

Stage Three

Two actors stand up and face each other. As before, one actor starts by observing some behaviour in the other actor and the other actor responds by repeating that observation but changing the pronoun. This continues until one actor is compelled by the other's behaviour to change the text entirely. For instance, the two actors are repeating 'You're crossing your arms,' 'I'm crossing my arms,' until one person is compelled to say, 'You're smiling.' At this point the other actor has to respond to this new observation and say, 'I'm smiling', and then both actors use this new text until one of them has the impulse to change it again.

The actors don't make these text changes happen; the text changes happen to the actors. They fly out like birds released from their cages, conscious only of their limitless freedom.

As before, the change in text should always be in response to something that is observed in the other person, it should never be forced. In fact, it's perfectly fine not to change the text at all. The actors should continue to respond to everything they observe in each other and only change the text when they feel compelled to do so.

It's quite difficult to get the balance right to start with, because once the actors are given permission to change the text, they want to do it all the time. This can be monitored by asking the rest of the group if they feel the changes were being imposed rather than being spontaneous.

It's also important to point out that these observations should not be about emotions. If someone were to say, 'You're making me angry,' they would be thinking about themselves and that would be missing the point of the exercise. They should be trying to connect with the other person, not thinking about their own feelings. Of course, one of the actors could actually be getting angry, but then they would let that anger come out in the simple repetition of the text, as in 'You're playing with your pen.' It could be possible to observe 'You're getting angry', but that would only muddy the issue, because the other person would have to repeat 'I'm getting angry,' and then they would be talking about their own emotions. If one person has an instinctive response to the other person's anger, then that person should observe the other's *behaviour* and not their *emotion*, as in 'You're shouting.'

This third stage is what I will now refer to a repetition exercise, and it is what we have been working towards. The fine-tuning of this exercise takes time – probably several sessions – but repetition is the bedrock of Meisner work, and once it is learned, it can be practised on a regular basis like barre exercises. It can also be used to explore the emotional subtext of a scene and to get the actors to connect with each other at any time during the rehearsal process.

Each repetition exercise usually lasts about two minutes, but later on, when the exercise is embedded in their psyche, two actors can clarify a moment of connection by doing the exercise for only as long as it is necessary. Sometimes ten or fifteen seconds will be enough.

Repetition is very exposing, because the actors are letting their own emotions take over. They are not being polite. In fact, they shouldn't be polite. They have permission to be impolite! And they should definitely take things personally. It should really matter to them. This will make it feel extremely real because it *is* extremely real. So if two people have been shouting at each other during the exercise, they should check that they are still okay with each other when they have finished. Similarly, if two people have been feeling very intimate as they do the exercise, they should make sure that there is no misunderstanding about their relationship when the exercise is over.

Meisner is about the two actors and the present moment. And that moment creates a subconscious response that becomes the next moment. It's like when two people are having a fight and one of them stubs their toe, which makes them both start laughing. The fight is forgotten as the laughter takes over. They connect from moment to moment.

It is unrealistic to think that the two actors are totally connected with each other 100% of the time. 10% of their attention will be on the knowledge that they are in a rehearsal room, on the stage or in front of the camera, and 10% will be tuning in to outside responses. And it is that 20% of external focus that keeps them safe. It stops them falling off the stage or walking into the camera. And it gives them a certain amount of control. But ultimately the other 80% of their attention will be fully on the other person, and 0% will be in control of their own impulsive responses.

Back-to-Back Repetition

Two actors do the repetition exercise, but standing back to back so they can't see each other.

This exercise helps each actor make a deep connection with the other actor, because their focus has to be on the most subtle manifestations of thought and emotion. But there is no such thing as nothing. Even if one actor is compelled to say, 'You're not moving,' they will be having an emotional response to the fact that they can't detect anything from the other person, and that will get the ball rolling.

Silent Repetition

Two actors face each other and do the repetition exercise without words, so they are both making a physical response to each other.

This exercise is the polar opposite of the previous exercise because the actors are now responding only to what they can see rather than what they can hear. As they tune in to the unconscious physical messages that they send to each other, their physical responses become automatic and unconsidered.

The Givens

This is short for the 'given circumstances', but since I have used that expression in a slightly differently context earlier in the book, I will shorten it to 'the givens' when talking about the Meisner technique.

When the actors have learned to give full attention to each other and to respond impulsively, the next stage is to colour the repetition exercise by making specific preparations and having objectives. These are called the 'givens', and they are how the actors create character. Their transformation has nothing to do with wigs, make-up and funny walks; it is internal. In fact, it is simply themselves working under a specific set of circumstances.

Preps

One actor stands outside the door and gets connected with an emotion while another actor does the same thing inside the room. When the person inside the room is ready, he or she shuts the door as a signal that they are ready to start. Then, when the person outside the room is also ready, they knock on the door, enter, and the two actors begin the repetition exercise.

This first given is to do with the feelings or emotions that the actors can connect with. Happiness, stress, anger, sadness... Whatever they like. In order to do this, they can tell themselves a story, remember an experience from their own lives or use any other method that works best for them. The important thing is to find a key that will stimulate a real emotion. Something that presses their buttons.

As soon as the actors meet, they should each give their full attention to the other person. They don't exactly drop their prep, but their response to the other actor is coloured by their prepped emotion. For instance, if one person has prepped to be really upset and the other person has prepped to be blissfully happy, then each will immediately be affected by the other person's behaviour. They see the world through the eyes of their emotion, but their attention is fully on the other person, and that is what they are responding to.

This exercise is not an end in itself, it is simply to train actors to work truthfully under a single given circumstance. Eventually, the technique will be applied to specific texts, and the preps will be appropriate to whatever character the actor is playing.

Knowledge

After the actors have prepped, but before they start their repetition, each is given a piece of information about the other person. (This information is invented by the director: it is not the truth.)

Specific knowledge about the characters will ultimately come from the script, but at this stage an extra bit of information about the other person will add another layer to the repetition exercise. The actors can be told things about each other like 'Chris really fancies you' or 'You've just overheard Hannah slagging you off'. So when they begin the repetition exercise, each person will see the other through the eyes of this new piece of information. They won't know what the other person has been told, so they will often start misreading each other. This is how a scene starts to develop.

Although this 'scene' still consists of the basic repetition exercise with words that are virtually meaningless, the underlying emotional connection and reaction will continue to be real and immediate.

Misreading and Projection

Two actors leave the room and the rest of the group stay in the room. The actors outside the room are asked to imagine that the rest of the group are all police officers. The actors inside the room don't know this, they are just asked to be themselves. When the two outsiders come into the room, the inside group must pretend that they don't know them and start asking them questions.

This exercise can be repeated with the actors outside the room being told that the group inside the room are all small children, or casting directors, or sports stars, etc.

Whatever the actors outside the room are told, they will behave accordingly. For instance, if they imagine that they are meeting a group of police officers they may get defensive when they are asked questions. This could lead to the rest of the group getting more authoritarian to try to get answers. If the actors coming into the room believe they are meeting small children, they will probably be happy to answer questions and they will make sure their answers are simple and easy to understand. At this point, the group inside the room, who are being treated like children, will start to behave like children. They respond to suit the behaviour of the other two actors, even though they have no idea what they are supposed to be.

This exercise prepares the actors for the next given.

As Ifs

After the actors have prepped, they are asked to do the repetition exercise as if the other person were someone else.

This given is to do with our behaviour patterns. We all have different versions of ourselves depending on who we are with. Different people bring about unconscious changes in our behaviour. Changes that we often don't even notice.

So the repetition exercise could be done as if the other person were the actor's brother. Or their ex-boyfriend. Or their girlfriend's father.

This exercise could also be done as if the other person were a specific type, like a bank manager or a hired killer, but whatever 'as if' is selected, the actor must apply it to the other actor and not think about their own behaviour.

When they do this, each actor changes the way they behave to suit the selected 'as if', but at the same time they are responding to the way the other person is treating them, because they too will be using an 'as if'. When both actors apply their 'as ifs', a complex scene will start to unfold.

And they are still just doing the repetition exercise. 'You're scratching your nose', 'I'm scratching my nose.'

Objectives

During the repetition exercise, each actor has to get the other actor to do something.

The actors can only use the words of the repetition exercise, but as they do it they have to try to make the other person jump, or leave the room, or sit on the floor. Whatever they want. They can't use any words about these activities, but each actor must be entirely focused on the other in order to see if their objectives are going well or badly.

For instance, if one person has decided that their objective is to get the other person to leave the room, and the other person isn't walking towards the door as soon as the repetition exercise starts, then the objective is not going well. So there has to be some sort of tactic to make the other person move. This tactic can be really bold. Maybe the person with the objective could walk towards the door themselves to see if the other person will follow. If the other person makes even the tiniest movement towards the door that will be a positive thing, and it will bring about a positive response. Each person has to be totally focused on the other so as to pick up the slightest indication whether their objective is going well or badly.

When the repetition exercise starts, it's important that the actors go straight for their objective. There's no point in holding back or waiting to build towards it. They must try to achieve their objective *now*!

Stakes

During a repetition exercise, each actor should think of a strong reason why they need to achieve their objective. They should try to make it truly matter for themselves; the stakes should be really high.

If an objective is actually important, then it raises the stakes and gives dynamism to the exercise. At the same time there will be close attention on the other person to see if the objective is being achieved. If it isn't, then the tactics will have to be changed immediately. There is no point in pursuing a plan of action if it is not getting any results. It's like a child trying to get their parents to buy them a toy. Although this objective has extremely high stakes for the child, they will never continue with a tactic that is not paying off. If pleading doesn't work, then maybe sulking will do the trick. If that's not working, how about smiling sweetly. Or flattering. Actually, children are quick to learn how to employ the right tactics to manipulate their parents!

So if the actors raise the stakes of an objective they automatically have to tune in to each other's responsive behaviour. Even from a distance. Imagine that you are at a party and there is someone you really fancy over the other side of the room. It doesn't matter what else is going on, or who you are talking to, you are totally tuned in to everything that the person you fancy is doing, because the stakes are high for you. You are making the connection because it's important to you.

The Four Givens

The four basic givens that the actors will use when they start working with a script are:

Preps:	'How am I feeling?'
As Ifs:	'Who is the other person?'
Objectives:	'What do I want from them?'
Stakes:	'Why is it important to me?'

These givens will bring a scene to life, but they can only work if each actor is taking their attention away from themselves and giving it to the other actor.

Actors should get out of their heads and live truthfully under a given set of circumstances.

12

Meisner in Application

CAESAR. If you apply yourself to our intents,
Which towards you are most gentle, you shall find
A benefit in this change…

Antony and Cleopatra (5.2)

ALL THE ACTING EXERCISES IN THE WORLD ARE POINTLESS if they are not part of the process of creating a performance. There is a big danger in thinking that drama classes are for the spiritual and psychological benefit of the actors themselves. But my interest lies in creating drama that tells stories either on the stage or in front of the camera. Stories that will enrich people's lives. Stories that are a window on the human condition. Stories that present the reality of the human condition so that members of the audience can reflect on their own lives.

Or on life itself.

The Meisner technique is specifically designed to bring those stories to life. Stories which are born in the minds of writers, nurtured through a solitary process of inspiration, hard work and technique, and finally emerge as a written text.

And it's this written text that is the creative starting point for actors.

Reading the Text

The actor's instinct when they first read a script is to experiment with various ways of performing the lines. They'll put on accents to suit the characters. They'll try out inflections. They'll want to bring extreme emotions like anger or passion to life even as they read the text in the privacy of their own homes. They'll even start to alter their physicality as they sit there. They'll make gestures with their hands. They'll hunch their shoulders. They'll tilt their heads. I know all this. I was an actor.

But all these things are like trying to run before you can walk. It's far too early. Not only that, but the actor is standing outside the character making these decisions, whereas he or she needs to get inside the character, and that takes time. Actors should break themselves of this habit. They should try to read the script as if they weren't even going to be playing a part. They should read it like a novel and just take in the story.

Harvesting Information

Facts

As the actors read the text for a second time they should write a list containing any information that they can find about their character.

Some of these facts will be embedded in the text, as in 'My character is a queen', 'My character lives in Brooklyn.' But some of them will be ideas that the actor gleans from the text. Something that springs to mind but is not specifically stated, as in 'My character hates her husband', 'My character is lonely.' When unsupported ideas like this are added to a list of facts they should have a question mark written by them so they can be examined and discussed later on. Our instinctive ideas and observations often uncover subtle truths if we allow them the freedom to do so. And the seed of an instinctive idea can often be lost if it's not written down.

Knowledge

The actors should write a list containing everything that their character knows before the start of each scene.

This is not what the *actor* knows, but what the *character* knows. More facts. But it is important not to include things that the character discovers during the scene or later in the story. This list should be about the knowledge that the character has before they embark on a scene. Of course, there may be some things that are not revealed to the audience until later in the play. For instance, a character could turn out to be a murderer in the very last scene of a script without there being any indication of this earlier in the play. Although this fact is not mentioned until the very end, the character would know they had done the crime all the way through the play, so it would become part of the actor's list of knowledge before he or she enters in the earlier scenes.

As before, anything that isn't supported by the text should have a question mark by it for further discussion in rehearsals.

Actions

The actors should go through their dialogue and write a list of what their character is doing when they say each line.

This list should be written separately from the script so the actor can look at it and see if it reveals any patterns or repetitions of behaviour. These actions are not the same as 'actioning the text' as described in Chapter 7; they are simply a description of what the character is actually doing. It should be straightforward and concise, without any deep thinking.

The following is a list of actions that can be applied to most lines of dialogue:

The character…

- Agrees about…
- Disagrees about…
- Asks a question about…
- Answers a question about…

- Answers a question with a question
- Greets
- Bids farewell
- Gives an order about…
- Thanks
- Apologises about…
- Gives an opinion about…
- Makes a suggestion about…
- Makes a comment about…
- Makes a statement about…
- Listens
- Stays silent
- Tells a lie about…

Having made the list, it can be used as part of the discussions that will happen later.

Gaps and Links

The actors should look at their lists and write down any links to their own lives that could be made with each item on the list. If there doesn't appear to be a link, they should mark it as a gap.

If the lists are regarded as a bunch of clues, then it is now possible for the actor to make a personal connection with some of these clues. There will be obvious connections that can simply be linked to their own lives. For instance, if the character has a brother and the actor has a brother then that is a shared experience that the actor can tap into when they are playing the scene.

Sometimes it will be necessary to think laterally and imaginatively. For instance, if an actress is playing Queen Gertrude in *Hamlet*, it is very unlikely that she will make a direct connection with that fact of being a queen, so she should ask herself what a queen actually does. She probably wears fabulous clothing, so maybe the actress can make a connection with that fact. A queen tells people what to do, so maybe a link can be made with something that the actress does in her own life. Maybe she has been a teacher, or the leader of a group. A queen often has a very busy diary. Does the actor have a busy diary too? If so, there is another link. This may seem simplistic, but it's all part of a build-up of connections.

After finding all these links there will still be gaps in the actor's connections with their character and these can be filled in a number of ways:

- **Improvisation:** This can give actors an experience that they might not have had before. For instance in the case of the actress playing the part of a queen, a simple exercise where everyone else in the group has to do what the queen demands will give the actress a connection with the feeling of unquestioned power.
- **Repetition:** This can be used to explore unfamiliar relationships. For instance, the actress could do a repetition as if the other actor were a servant.
- **Shared knowledge:** This can help to fill in the gaps. For instance, one actor might be able to tell another actor about an experience in their life that will help that actor understand some aspect of their character and that will help them make the connection to a gap in their lists.

Discussion

The director and the actors should have an open discussion about all the information that they have harvested from their lists.

This should be a discussion about the actors' discoveries, not about the actual text. These discoveries will become part of the givens, but at this stage they should not suggest a way of saying the lines. The discussion is to enable the actors to share as much information as possible. Ultimately, it will help them make decisions and choices. During this discussion each actor should add any new thoughts that they have to their lists.

Decisions and Choices

The actors should make decisions and choices about their characters. These choices should be the ones that are most interesting and exciting for the actors.

Having harvested the facts and analysed them through discussion, each actor can now make decisions that will bring their character to life. The discussion may alter some of the decisions – and the actors are free to change their minds – but they should not try to resolve differences of opinion if they don't feel like it, because that will dilute their point of view.

When these discussions don't produce incontestable truths, the actor has to make choices. A character may say they love someone, but do they really? They may be lying. The actor has to make the choice even when the other actors don't agree. One actor may decide that she has been married for ten years, while the actor playing her husband may decide that they have been married for three years. Unless there is dialogue about this fact in the script, it can't be resolved. But it doesn't matter, because for the wife it will feel like a ten-year marriage, and for the husband it will feel like a three-year marriage. That's life. Time feels different to different people.

No one in real life feels the same as other people about everything. Each actor's decision is a gold nugget and they don't have to share it with anyone else. It is theirs. They should value it and own it with pride.

Creating the Givens

Using all the information they have gathered so far, including the decisions and choices, the actors then create the four givens for a particular scene.

These givens are exactly the same as the ones the actors used when they learned how to do the repetition exercise (see Chapter 11), but now, rather than observing and responding *from their own point of view*, they can do the repetition exercise by observing and responding *through the eyes of their character.*

The four givens are:

- A prep
- An objective
- Stakes
- An 'As if'

I put these in a slightly different order in the last chapter, because that was the best way to learn about them. When they are used as part of the work on a text, the order above is a better progression.

Testing the Givens

The repetition exercise can now be used to test each of the four givens.

Taking them one at a time, each given can be tested and altered until it feels more or less appropriate for the scene. I say 'more or less' because there is never a perfect version of the givens waiting to be discovered. There is never a perfect version of a scene. There is never a perfect version of a play. There is only the version that is happening *now*. Though sometimes one version does feel better than the others. Actors should never strive for the Holy Grail of perfection, they should just keep searching for it. But if something feels good, then they are probably on the right lines.

A Prep

Although the prepped emotion should be something that has a connection with the character's state at the beginning of a scene, the way the actor achieves that emotional state doesn't have to have anything to do with the character or the scene. For instance, in Act One, Scene Seven of Shakespeare's *Macbeth*, Lady Macbeth confronts Macbeth because he is having doubts about killing Duncan. The scene starts when she says, 'He has almost supp'd. Why have you left the chamber?' Now the actress could decide that Lady Macbeth's emotion at this point is extremely angry, so as a prep she should think of something in her own life that makes her feel angry. It could be something as mundane as shopping in a supermarket, or political like the way the Government funds the Social Services, it doesn't matter. But whatever it is, it has to be something that really makes the actress angry when she thinks about it.

This prep should only take about ten minutes, although practised actors can often key into a prepped emotion very quickly. Sometimes in only half a minute or so.

Having prepped the appropriate emotion for their character, the actors then do the repetition exercise. They are not using the words of the scene; they are simply doing a straightforward repetition, as in 'You're blinking', 'I'm blinking.'

If the mood of the repetition feels more or less like the mood of the scene, the actors can move on to testing an objective. If it doesn't feel like the scene, they can try other preps until they feel as if they are in the right area.

An Objective

The objective should be the character's objective in the scene, and it should be made a simple as possible. For instance, in the scene above, where Lady Macbeth is trying to get Macbeth to murder Duncan, then it would be impossible to achieve that objective during a repetition exercise. But if the objective is something as simple as trying to get the other actor to stand near them, then that is achievable. The actress would still be trying to get the other actor to do something. It would be a simple objective. Don't forget that the other actor will have an objective as well.

The two actors do their preps and then use the repetition exercise to test their objectives. As before, they can try different objectives until one feels more or less like the right one for the scene.

These repetitions vary in length. Sometimes they can be only thirty seconds or so, and sometimes they can be up to five or even ten minutes. This is because the whole point is to test the givens until they feel more or less right, and once that happens, there is no need to carry on with the exercise.

Stakes

The actors need to raise the stakes of their objectives in order to give the repetition exercise all the emotional and subtextual ingredients of the scene. By doing this, they will be making the right connections as they focus in on each other. They will be experiencing the appropriate emotions, they will have strong objectives, and they will be giving appropriate responses. In the case of the scene from *Macbeth*, Lady Macbeth's objective could be to get Macbeth to stand near her, so she could raise the stakes by feeling that if he moves even the slightest bit towards her, it would be proof that he really loves her (positive stake); or if he doesn't move at all, she's lost him for ever (negative stake). But whatever stakes an actor chooses, they must make it something that really matters for them.

An 'As If'

The actors can now add the 'as ifs' if they need to. Sometimes it's not necessary because they may already have started to make the right connections, but if not, they can do the repetition exercise as if the other actor was their boyfriend, or their teacher, etc. Anything that they might think is appropriate to the way the characters feel about each other. To continue with the example from *Macbeth*, Lady Macbeth could do the repetition as if Macbeth were a small child, or as if he were the actress's own father, or the person she loves most in the world. As with all these choices, it has to be something that really matters for the actor.

Discussion

After all four givens have been tested, the actors can have another discussion about what feels right or wrong. It can be quite hard for each actor to know whether their choice of givens is creating the right story, because the repetition exercise is the coming together of two actors with two different sets of givens. If the actors' choices don't seem to be telling the right story then they can be encouraged to test different givens until the repetition exercise feels something like the scene.

When they have discovered appropriate and useful preps, objectives, stakes and 'as ifs', the actors should write them down. These are the conditions of the scene itself.

Conditions

The actors are in charge of these conditions, and they can be tested and changed at any time to add other layers to a scene, but each time they are changed they should be written down. Naturally, the conditions affect the repetition, and that will affect the scene. How the actors feel is a result of these conditions. How they respond is coloured by these conditions. And when something matters, it matters because of these conditions.

The conditions create the character. The actors are not putting on their characters, they are becoming their characters. 'Character' is the actor him or herself living under a particular set of conditions. For instance, if an actor is playing a doctor, then he is not trying to discover some stereotypical version of how a doctor should behave, he is behaving as himself if he had become a doctor. Yes, he may put on a white coat, but it's still just the actor himself up there. There is no one else.

This is an important concept when using this technique, so I'll say it again.

A character is simply the actor living under a particular set of conditions.

(This may appear to be in direct opposition to some of the explorations in previous chapters, but it isn't really because we have yet to add the actual lines of dialogue and the externals.)

When actors do the repetition exercise under the specific conditions of a particular scene, the rest of the group can see it come to life. They see the responsive, emotional connection between two characters living in the moment, and that is the essence of a scene.

But although the group saw the scene come alive, they didn't hear the dialogue that's in the script, and the actors ultimately need to speak the dialogue in order to perform the play or the film. Although the repetition exercise may feel like the scene, there is one missing ingredient and that is, of course, the actual text.

The Dialogue

'At last!' you cry. And that is totally understandable because everything starts with the dialogue. But the dialogue is often just a surface expression of the underlying dynamics of a scene. The real meaning of the scene is often in the subtext, and the essence of a scene can exist without the words. But let's face it, scriptwriters choose to tell a story largely by making the characters talk to each other, and it's the actors' job to make that dialogue come to life. That's the most important thing. That's what analysis, research and repetition are all about. They are simply to bring life to the dialogue, so the audience feels they are watching something close to reality. That's what makes a story interesting for an audience. That's what makes it spring to life before their very eyes.

Learning the Lines

The actors learn their lines on their own. As they learn them, they should not try to make sense of them. They should learn them without meaning. The meaning only comes when they are responding to each other.

This is a difficult way to learn lines, but it is an essential part of the process, because, as I said, the essence of a scene is not in the words that are spoken; it is in the connection between the actors.

As they learn their lines on their own, the actors should find different ways to break any kind of vocal pattern that might start to emerge. There are several ways they can do that.

They can run their lines:

- Flat
- Up and down the scale
- Like a robot
- At speed
- Moving around
- Washing up
- Doing press-ups
- Shadow-boxing
- Juggling
- Taking a step on each word as they walk down the street

Running the Words of a Scene

Once they have learned their lines, the actors run the words of a scene together, playing a lively physical game with each other. They can use children's playground games like skipping or clapping hands. If a whole group of actors is working on a scene together, they can play games like 'Tag' or 'Stuck in the Mud' as they speak the dialogue.

The actors should only run their lines with each other when they are totally confident that they know them. They should avoid making eye contact, because that will make them start to respond to each other, and it's important that the actors know the lines inside out before they make any connections.

As they run their lines, the actors need to be totally free from preconceptions. The words should be springing from their mouths spontaneously, without consideration, just as they do in real life. So a game that involves them concentrating on specific patterns of movement or running around the room is perfect. They won't have time to think, and the words will just pour out. Actors should be able to run their lines while they are cooking a meal, playing a game on a PlayStation, building a model of the *Cutty Sark* out of matchsticks, or sweeping the floor.

At every stage of the rehearsal period, lines should be run as a technical exercise before any scene is rehearsed. There should be no eye contact and the actors should have a physical activity as they run them.

The Cues

The actors run the lines, making sure they are confident that they know their cues.

It's often the case that actors know their lines extremely well without knowing exactly when to say them. They haven't learned their cues. So there is a game the actors can do to make sure they are sharp on picking up their cues.

Still without eye contact, the actors run their lines, grabbing a cushion back and forth immediately they hear their cue. They can only say their lines when they have got the cushion, and there must be no pauses. This helps them concentrate on what the other person is saying and makes them really listen for their moment to speak.

Adding Words to the Repetition Exercise

The actors use the four givens of the scene – preps, objectives, stakes and 'as ifs' – but instead of doing the repetition exercise, they say the lines of the text.

The actors should still not try to make sense of the words. They should just play the conditions and let the words come out of their mouths. They should not even try to be appropriate to what they think the text is all about. And if they start 'acting' the sense of the words, they should go straight back to the repetition exercise in order to connect with each other and not the text inside their heads.

If they are connecting with each other correctly, then the words will automatically start to make sense, but the text should only float over the surface of the connection. The words don't matter. The connection does.

It is important that the actors realise that they are not 'doing the scene' at this point, otherwise they will want to start 'acting'. However, they will eventually realise that the connection *is* the scene.

Meaning

If the text is difficult to understand, then the actors should go through the text together, looking up everything that they don't understand and writing down the actual meaning in their own words.

Up until this point, the text has been treated as a bunch of meaningless words, but now it is time for the actors to understand exactly what they are saying. They also need to know exactly what they are listening to, so the meaning of difficult texts should be discussed with the whole group. Eventually, everyone should know exactly what everything means.

Paraphrasing

Now they know the text and have a thorough understanding of what it means, the actors stand opposite each other and improvise the scene using only the words that they themselves would use.

This is to ensure a complete understanding of the text – particularly if the play is written in heightened language. When the actors have finished this exercise, it is worth discussing why the writer has chosen to use particular words for a character to speak. The actors should also discuss the way the characters speak on different occasions. For instance, a character may use half-finished sentences connected by dots at some points during a scene, and free-flowing, complete sentences at other points. If that is the case, the actor needs to decide why the writer has chosen to change the character's speech patterns during the scene. The actors might also notice that their character has a particular way of speaking when they are lying, or that different sentence structures indicate that their character is either confident or unsure of themselves.

A discussion about the choice of words and the particular phrasing that characters use can lead to more observations being made. It can change the givens. It can lead to different choices or strengthen the choices that have already been made.

Back to Back

The actors prep the scene, think about the givens, and then speak the text, standing back to back.

This helps the actors really tune in to each other. As they listen, they hear everything the other person says through the filter of their own objective. They are so focused on the other person that they are not worrying about themselves, and as a result their words will often come out brilliantly. They are not thinking about their own text, and yet their words start to zing with life because they are making the right connections.

Using the Words

The actors face each other and, after prepping the four givens, they use the words to try to achieve their objectives.

Although the actors can start using their lines to achieve their objectives, they must still let their reaction come from an impulse that is driven by their connection with the other actor. Again, if they start to 'act' their words, they should prep the four givens and go back to the simple repetition exercise.

Heads Against the Wall

The actors face each other across the room with their heads touching the wall behind them. They prep the scene and then speak the text, using the words to try to achieve their objectives from a distance.

This is similar to the above rehearsal exercise, except the distance between them forces them to do two things. Firstly, they really have to concentrate on each other in order to make a connection; and secondly, they have to ensure that they are using their words powerfully enough to achieve their objectives from a distance. The words are their only weapon. They speak with how they feel.

The Externals

So far we have been working on the inner life of the character, but now it is time to add some necessary external aspects that are dictated either by the script or by the actor's own personal choices made during the creative process. Some of these 'externals' will have been developed independently during the rehearsal period, but so far they will not have been incorporated into the repetition exercises or the text work.

Accents

The actors start using the appropriate accent for their character when they work on the scene.

Up to this point, all the repetition exercises and the scene work will have been done in the actor's own accent, but if a character has a specific accent then the actor should have learnt that accent separately. They may have had help from a voice coach or they may have listened to accent recordings, but whatever their approach they should have practised the accent with other texts and not the script they are working on.

But now they can start to apply the accent to the scene.

As soon as they do that, the actors will often go into their own heads. They will start thinking about themselves again and not connecting with each other. This is to be expected. To help them overcome that problem they should do a repetition exercise using the accent, and then go straight back to doing the scene.

The trick is for them not to focus on their own accent but to respond to the other character's accent.

Physical Posture

The actors can now add physical mannerisms or postures to their character when they run the scene.

The actors may have discovered various physical mannerisms for their character when they were doing their repetitions, as in 'leading from their heads' or 'lifting their shoulders'. These can now become part of the scene. But as before, if they start going into their own heads, they should immediately do a repetition exercise. And it's the same advice as for the accents: they should focus on the other actor's physicality and not on their own.

Stage Directions

Any moves or activities that are indispensable can now be added to the scene.

Most of the stage directions in the script can be ignored. In fact, it is often useful for the actors to cross out all the stage directions in the script before they start work on it. Each actor should find the impulse to move as a response to the other actor, or from the need to achieve their objective. They should only move if something makes them want to move.

However, there are some moves or activities that are vital to the scene. It would be impossible to put on an effective production of Sam Shepard's *Fool for Love* without the actors continually slamming the door when they come in and out of the room. It's part of the drama and the mood of the play (the set constructors have to build a really solid set in order for this play to work properly!). The taking, giving and lighting of cigarettes is essential to the mood of a Noël Coward play, and however unfashionable smoking has become, the scenes lose something if the actors don't use cigarettes at certain times. Gwendolen has to drink tea during Act Two of *The Importance of Being Earnest*, and Algernon has to eat cucumber sandwiches during Act One. These are external givens, and the actors have to incorporate them into the scene.

There are also moves and activities that the actors are given by the director for reasons of clarity or for effect. These too have to be incorporated. It's no good saying, 'My character wouldn't do that,' if the director wants your character to do it. The move should become one of the externals of a scene. Of course, actors should always find the impulse for a move for themselves, ideally in response to something outside themselves. But if all else fails, *they should just do it*!

Costume

The actors should put on their costumes and then do the repetition exercise.

This is to see how the costumes affect the actors and, of course, to see how they each respond to the other actors' costumes.

Costumes have a powerful effect on actors, and initially they will go into their own heads when they first put them on. But the repetition exercise will help them to reconnect with each other until the costume becomes part of the scene.

Technical Rehearsals

If the actors have to run the scene during a technical rehearsal, or while practising a fight sequence or at any other time during the final days of rehearsal, they should either run the words technically without meaning or they should work under the four givens. They should never try to act the scene properly without the givens because that will take them back into their own heads.

Putting on the Show

The first night of a show is a scary event, and when people are scared they immediately want to be in control. The trouble is, if the actors get fearful and try to take control of their performance during the first night of a play that has been rehearsed using the Meisner technique, they will be trying to do the scene in a way that has literally *never been rehearsed*. So it is very unlikely that it will be any good. The actors have to learn to 'fall into each other' as they have been doing during the rehearsal period. They have to say to themselves:

'I do not know what I am about to do and I'm pleased about that. I have no idea how the scene will unfold and I will embrace that.'

All the work so far will give the actors everything they need to perform a dynamic and truthful version of the text. They will be acting on impulse and that will make the audience really connect with the story. If they trust this work, the scenes will tell themselves.

This particular training is to get the actors out of their heads. If at any point during a performance they feel themselves going back into their own heads and they feel they are consciously 'acting', then all they have to do is to concentrate on what the other people in the scene are doing and everything will fall into place without them having to do anything else.

This requires trust in themselves. Trust in each other. And trust of the process.

It's a risk and it's a true leap of faith, but it's a sure way of making a play come to life for the audience.

Epilogue

PROSPERO. … be cheerful, sir:
Our revels now are ended. These our actors,
As I foretold you, were all spirits and
Are melted into air, into thin air:
And, like the baseless fabric of this vision,
The cloud-capp'd towers, the gorgeous palaces,
The solemn temples, the great globe itself.
Yea, all which it inherit, shall dissolve
And, like this insubstantial pageant faded,
Leave not a rack behind. We are such stuff
As dreams are made on…

The Tempest (4.1)

THERE ARE MANY DIFFERENT TECHNIQUES DESCRIBED IN this book and they are not always compatible. Some will appeal to some actors, and others to others. But all the techniques can be useful in helping actors to develop their skills, prepare their performances and present their stories with truth.

Actors stimulate their audiences' imagination and deepen their perception of human nature. They make them laugh at life's ironies and they make them cry at life's misfortunes. They can scare their audiences and they can keep them on the edge of their seats. They can edify them and they can make them ponder. They entertain them and they educate them. For a brief couple of hours, actors are the ringmasters of the audiences' emotions as they take them on a journey into their imaginations.

And although one or two actors get enormous acclaim and become regular chat-show guests and gossip-column celebrities, most of them just do their job when they can and share the applause with the rest of the cast.

But what a job it is, and what a responsibility!

Luckily, the general public are completely unaware of the work that goes into preparing a performance, and it would spoil things if they did. The Wizard of Oz seems to be a fantastic, magical figure, but when Dorothy draws back the curtain and reveals the real man frantically operating the controls, her sense of wonder disappears. We don't want the audience to lose their sense of wonder. We want them to enjoy the magic as much as the actors do.

And we want them to experience the fantastic world and the multifarious people in it as they really are.

Good luck
to anyone and everyone who enjoys acting!

Index of Exercises

Also by John Abbott

THE IMPROVISATION BOOK

A practical guide to conducting improvisation sessions, for teachers, directors and workshop leaders.

The Improvisation Book takes you step-by-step, session-by-session through a graded series of improvisation exercises. Starting with the very first class, it adds a new element at each stage until even the most inhibited students have gained a full vocabulary of improvisational techniques. The book comes with a set of cut-out-and-keep cards to use in workshops and rehearsals.

'A veritable treasure trove... Abbott's book is of real value in the training of actors; I'm enthused and excited about putting it into practice' *ReviewsGate.com*

IMPROVISATION IN REHEARSAL

An indispensable introduction to how theatre directors at every level can use improvisation in the rehearsal room.

Packed with useful exercises and improvisation scenarios, and drawing examples from a wide variety of plays, *Improvisation in Rehearsal* reveals how improvisation enriches and enlivens the creation of characters, back-stories, relationships, shared histories and emotional lives. As Mark Rylance says in his Foreword, this book **'will inspire and delight its readers'**.

'There is little doubt that Abbott's books will be compulsory reading for many directors and actors long into the future' *British Theatre Guide*

Available from www.nickhernbooks.co.uk
and all good bookshops